Maine Lighthouses

A Pictorial Guide

West Quoddy Head Light - Lubec, Maine

Maine Lighthouses

A Pictorial Guide

Courtney Thompson

**Designed, edited and published by
CatNap Publications**

ISBN: 0-9651786-9-2
Library of Congress Catalog Card Number: 00-093709

Photography and text: Courtney Thompson

Maps and line graphics:
Wesley A. Shaw, Ripples Graphics
Mt. Desert, ME. 04660

Additional photos by:
Ted & Jo Panayotoff : Page 50- top right, bottom left, Page 51 right top & center, bottom left,
Page 71 bottom left, Page 73 middle left, Page 84 middle right
Chris Mills: Page 26 top left, Page 27 top & middle right
Jeremy D'Entremont : Page 84 middle right; Page 114 top left, bottom right; Page 120

Printed in Canada by Quebecor Atlantic
St. John, New Brunswick Canada

For purchase information please contact:
CatNap Publications
P.O. Box 848   Mt. Desert, Maine 04660
(207) 244-0485

For my father. His forethought and love made this project possible.

Table of Contents

Penobscot Bay

Midcoast

Kennebec & Boothbay Area

Casco Bay

Casco Bay(con't)

NOTE: Information contained in the light list tables and individual maps is not intended for navigational purpose. Consult appropriate nautical charts

Introduction

A lighthouse can be at once peaceful, lonely, beautiful, forlorn, silent and raucous, signaling both welcome and warning. While often subject to harsh, unforgiving conditions, lighthouses also enjoy locations of breathtaking beauty. However, the benevolent appearance of the lighthouse under clear skies and calm seas often becomes a presence of foreboding and loneliness when dense fog and rough seas dominate. Lighthouses which host summer visitors, in winter become wonderfully deserted and peaceful; those which in summer offer a challenging, appealing destination for vacationing sailors, become isolated and lonely, facing winter's storms head on.

Primarily, however, a lighthouse represents stability and certainty; therein lies a strength of purpose which many find in them. Although the character of the sea constantly changes, the lighthouse provides a constant point of reference. It's noted that the technical function of the lighthouse is no longer needed for navigation, but clearly the intangible elements and attraction cannot be replaced.

This book is intended to present a comprehensive guide to the lighthouses of Maine. What began as a personal goal to visit, document and photograph each light turned into a project of unexpected scope. While travelling the coast of Maine, I found books which included photographs, directions, and historical notes in varied combination. However, none of the available titles provided a complete compilation of varied photographs, general information/history, directions and a small map of the immediate area. Therefore, my objective was the collection of these elements into one volume. The second edition offers new and additional photographs for each light, historic images, expanded narrative material and updated directions. The historic images are intended to suggest a glimpse into the past when the lighthouses all were vital, functioning and peopled; dating is noted when possible.

In order to visit, revisit and photograph the Maine lighthouses, I followed well-travelled routes, meandered back roads, explored peninsulas, coves and islands. I was able to experience the beauty of the Maine coast from land, sea and air. Moreover, the many people I met during this adventure were friendly, helpful and patient; all were accommodating and understanding when the vagaries of coastal weather caused unexpected changes or improvisation in schedule, routes and plans.

The following individuals provided invaluable assistance. Ted and Jo Panayotoff, lighthouse enthusiasts and innkeepers, graciously let me join their lighthouse cruises, offered postcards from their collection for use in the book and provided valuable editorial advice. The Maine portion of the Introductory Section was written from material researched and prepared by Ted; his knowledge, enthusiasm and contributions were instrumental in preparation of this edition. Jeremy D'Entrement generously offered material which was instrumental in revision and expansion of the narrative notes. These contributions were reflected in the significant additions and improvements seen in the second edition of this book in 1998. Since then, implementation of the Maine Lights initiative has resulted in many significant, positive changes with the lighthouses in this program; extensive repairs and renovations are underway and will be ongoing at many locations. This edition reflects, as possible, those improvements.

Finally, my thanks to all who helped me along the way, in whatever way.

The Lighthouse Tradition
Early History: Looking Back

Throughout most of recorded history lighthouses have not only aided mariners in navigation but also represented unique architectural reflections of cultural development. As man began to cross the seas and oceans to trade civilization spread; navigational aids were a mark of expanding explorations and technology. Lighthouses have evolved from fires burning on hilltops to modern masonry or steel-frame structures capable of resisting the severest storms.

Although the Phoenicians and Egyptians are thought to have built lighthouses, no records document their construction; priests likely were the first "lightkeepers", building bonfires at landfalls in Egypt. Completed in Alexandria, Egypt in the third century B.C., the Pharos of Alexandria is the first lighthouse which is documented with detailed accounts. The stone structure with wood fire on top was built c. 280 BC at the mouth of Alexandria Harbor and thought to be the world's first lighthouse. Thereafter, "pharos" came to mean "lighthouse"; the science of lighthouse construction and illumination became "pharology". Considered one of the Seven Wonders of the World, with elaborate carvings and ornamentation, for more than 1500 years the structure functioned as an aid to navigation, withstanding damage sustained by invaders and earthquakes, until it finally succumbed in the 14th century. As the Roman Empire spread across Europe, lighthouses followed; existence of more than 30 lighthouses throughout the widespread Roman provinces has been documented. Most coastal lights did not survive the Dark Ages although some monastic orders kept fires burning near their coastal monasteries. In some English parishes lights were placed in church towers, giving rise to the tradition that lighting the coasts was the work of Christian charity.

Early Eddystone tower

Trading among European nations increased at the end of the Dark Ages (about 1100), resulting in increased shipping activity and construction of more lighthouses particularly in England, France, Germany and Italy. The formalization of lighthouse service was a result of the suppression of monastic orders during the reign of Henry VIII. In 1565 the first statute dealing with lighthouses in Great Britain was enacted, creating the Corporation of the Trinity House. The law noted that the Corporation "*shall....erect and set up...beacons, marks and signs for the sea, in such place or places.....whereby dangers may be avoided and escaped and ships the better come into their ports without peril.*" Although a boon to mariners, the navigational aids were not welcomed by all coastal dwellers; those who depended on shipwrecks as a source of fuel and goods vocally opposed the construction of beacons. Nevertheless, the number of major lighthouses increased dramatically during the age of discovery and colonial trade in the 16th and 17th centuries.

Construction

The golden age of tower design was seen in the early centuries of lighthouse construction. Most Old World towers were of stone masonry construction, located at important ports. As rapid advances in equipment and construction occured in the 1700s, the first towers completely exposed to the sea were built-- notably the Eddystone Light fourteen miles offshore from the port of Plymouth, England. The successive forms of this structure mirrored increasingly scientific design principles.

In 1696-1699 a massive wooden tower was built on the rock, anchored by twelve iron stanchions. Destroyed by storm in 1703, the tower was rebuilt in 1708 in the form of a slender, tapering wooden structure built around a central timber mast. When this tower burned in 1755, it was replaced with masonry blocks dovetailed together to form a curved profile to resist wind and waves, a design which soon became standard. In 1882 the present lighthouse was built, nearly twice the height of the previous, resting on a solid masonry base, with foundation stones dovetailed into each other and into the reef. Lighthouses at other isolated spots were then patterned after Eddystone.

The 16th and 17th centuries saw rapid expansion of trade from Europe to the Americas, with construction of lighthouses in North America following the pattern seen in Europe. In both Canadian and American colonies, the first lights were located at important harbors-- the first in the United States in Boston Harbor, the first in Canada at Louisburg, Cape Breton. Both initial structures were destroyed by the British armies. Lighthouses and keeper's quarters in colonial America were primarily built of stone, with functionality and simplicity uppermost in design objectives. With a few exceptions, most lighthouses in the Atlantic colonies in Canada were built of wood. Availability of the resource and low cost enabled timely construction of wood structures. Given the harsh and damp marine climate, these structures proved surprisingly durable; the lighthouse at Gannet Rock in the Bay of Fundy has withstood the elements since construction in 1831.

Fuel & Illumination Systems

Most early lights were harbor lights, often so feeble that a vigorous debate arose whether lights should be used to warn mariners to steer clear of dangers or to guide them to a safe location. The argument was not without merit. In these early beacons, the source of light was typically an open fire atop the tower, subject to the elements. Fires were fueled by wood taken from the area, often eliminating the nearby forest in short order. Open fires, using wood or candles, were not generally reliable, often sputtering out or causing fires. Additionally, a strong wind determined the effectiveness of the light; blustery winds from the land produced brighter light to seaward, thus aiding mariners, whereas stiff sea breezes were likely to diminish the flame seen by mariners at sea. Rain also was a key factor, making presence of the flame erratic in storms; not until later years were lanterns enclosed, often with glazed material which also reduced the visibility of the light if not kept meticulously clean.

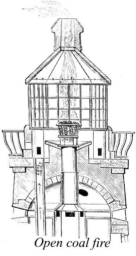

Open coal fire

Coal became standard after 1500 because it burned more slowly than wood and produced a better light. Wind was again a significant factor however. When buffeted by strong winds, coal fires often generated sufficient heat to melt or damage the grate container. During fog or rain it was however possible that the glow from the open fires might be reflected in the atmosphere much like the linger of the sun's glow at sunset. It wasn't until the middle of the 19th century that open coal fires were discontinued, the last extinguished in England in 1823.

Swiss-born Aime Argand is credited with a major technological advancement in illumination. The Argand lamp--an oil lamp with circular wick protected by glass chimney-- was invented in 1782 and was the principle lighthouse illuminant for more than a century. The lamp was combined with reflectors to produce a bright, concentrated light which was not diffused and thereby lost. Sperm oil was typically used as fuel, although others were tried with varying degrees of success, including seal, porpoise, and cod liver oil. Animal-based oils were later replaced by vegetable oils, such as colza, refined from rapeseed. A Canadian, Abraham Gesner, in 1846 made a further significant contribution to lighting technology with the invention of coal oil, or kerosene. Used in flat-wick lamps, kerosene was the standard illuminant until the turn of the century and the advent of petroleum and acetylene lamps. In the late 18th and early 19th century the incandescent oil vapor lamp came into use, creating a bright light well suited to the Fresnel lens.

Light beams are captured and concentrated by two means: the rays can be reflected with mirrors (catoptric principle) or they can be deflected by passing them through lenses (dioptric principle). Reflectors and refractors were designed to focus, or concentrate, the light into a single powerful beam. The catoptric reflector (1777) consisted of hundreds of mirror sections set in a plaster mold in the form of a parabolic curve. Silvered copper reflectors later replaced these. The resulting beam of light then had to be rotated by clockwork mechanism in order to be visible from any direction. Bowl-shaped mirrors of varying diameter were grouped behind the light to increase the power of an Argand lamp up to seven-fold. This apparatus could become cumbersome and often almost entirely filled the lantern room.

Reflector lamp

The next, and key, breakthrough in lighthouse optics was the introduction of lenses, specifically those designed by Augustin Fresnel. Fresnel was an engineer and pioneer in the study of optics. He began his research in 1814 and by 1822 had perfected the dioptric system, a lighthouse lens superior to anything previously developed. Glass prisms at the center of a bull's eye lens magnified the light, sending out a thin, horizontal beam of concentrated light. Fresnel later added reflecting prisms above and below, producing the catadioptric system, the basis of optical systems in lighthouses today. Illumination was originally from a lamp inside the lens; lamps for smaller lenses required one or two circular wicks with four or five required for larger lenses placed one inside the other.

The order or size of the Fresnel lens was determined by the distance of the flame from the lens, or focal distance. Numbered one through six, the first order lens had the greatest focal length, the sixth order the shortest. Similarly, the first order lens had the largest diameter and sixth the smallest. Used primarily in seacoast lights, the first-order Fresnel lens weighed up to six tons; the small fourth and fifth order lenses weighed 200-300 pounds. A fixed light was produced by a lens with smooth glass at its center belt; a glass molded into the form of a bull's eye at the center belt was used for a flashing light with rotation of the lens via clockwork mechanism producing the flashing effect. In 1890 a method was devised to rotate the lights by floating the apparatus on a bed of mercury, thereby virtually eliminating friction and permitting revolutions as frequently as every 15 seconds.

Identification

Improvements in lighting technology made the lights more visible and four international light classifications were defined according to size and intenstiy: landfall, major coastal, secondary coastal and harbor. However, for the mariner the problem of distinguishing between lighthouses, especially those relatively close together, was a significant one. Mistaking one light for another was often a fatal error. For identification in daylight hours, the structures were painted with disinctive "daymarks", typically colored stripes or bands, which made the lighthouse stand out from the land. White was found to show up best against land, even in snow; red or black stripes, bands or lantern rooms further distinguished a specific structure.

Accurate identification of the lights at night presented yet another challenge. Rotation of the light was the first intervention; placement of reflectors or screens caused the rotating light to flash or occult. A flashing light displays the beam for a shorter time than the subsequent period of darkness; the reverse pattern produces an occulting light. Rotation of the light was initially accomplished by a weight-driven clockwork mechanism, similar to that used in grandfather clocks. The keeper was required to wind the mechansim every few hours. The advent of the electric motor eliminated this tedious winding duty.

Early Fresnel rotating mechanism

Electrification of the lighthouse was the 20th century's most significant advance in lighting technology. High intensity electric lights, particularly the mercury vapor bulb, eliminated the need for elaborate ground glass prims and Fresnel lenses. Additionally batteries and solar power now have further streamlined illumination. Automation of all types of lights via computer is now standard practice although a few manned stations remain worldwide.

Lighting America's Coast

The first lighthouse in the United States was built in 1716 on Little Brewster Island at the entrance to Boston Harbor to serve merchant and maritime interests in the Massachusetts colony. Candles or lamps burning whale oil produced the first light atop the circular tower with spider lamps installed in the 1790s. Although the acrid fumes produced by these oil-burning lamps burned the keeper's nostrils, limiting his time in the lantern room, this type of illumination was standard in American lighthouses until the introduction of Winslow Lewis' lighting system.

Ten additional lighthouses were built in the colonies prior to the Revolution; afterward the individual states maintained control of their respective lighthouses and made necessary repairs to damage inflicted by the war. In 1789 the US Lighthouse Service was established when Congress assigned national responsibility for maintenance and all activity relative to aids to navigation when the federal government was established. States were required to cede their lighthouses and all aids to navigation to the Treasury Department and signature of the President was required for appointment of keepers until the mid 1800s. Local superintendents retained responsibility for daily activities and operation of lighthouses, construction and repair, selection of sites for new structures, acquisition of the land and collection of customs. For these added duties they were compensated with 2.5 percent of all revenue related to lighthouses in their area.

The lighthouse at Portland Head (ME) was the first put into service following the Congressional act, followed by Cape Henry (VA) in 1792. Trade in the New England area thrived following the Revolution and a boom in lighthouse construction accompanied this growth. During the period 1800-1810, fourteen of nineteen lighthouses built were in New England and New York; only three of these were coastal lights, the rest harbor lights. To a lesser degree increased trade traffic also prompted construction of lighthouses in southern waters during the next decade, but New England still led the nation. Several additional coastal lights were built (inlcuding those on Boon and Petit Manan Islands), but most were again located in harbors or bays. By 1820 fifty five lighthouses were in operation along the east coast. As maritime trade increased, so did lighthouse construction. New structures were built at a steady rate throughout the late 1800s and into the early 1900s.

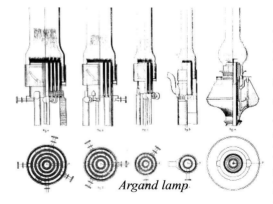

Argand lamp

As in Europe, oil lamps were used early on as illuminants for the light. These "spider" lamps consisted of a central oil reservoir (the body) and several projecting tubes (legs). Modeled after lighting systems used in England, the Argand lamp and parabolic reflector designed by Winslow Lewis became standard apparatus in early American lighthouses of the colonial period and early 1800s. Tests of this system at Boston Harbor light revealed the reflectors and lamps produced a light far superior to the spider lamps. Congress allotted $60,000 for purchase of Lewis' system, installation of the lights in all existing lighthouses and maintenance for a ten-year period. Lewis began installation in 1812, but was forced to interrupt his task during the War of 1812. He then completed the work in 1815 when fighting ceased. However, the lens used in the Argand lamps had a greenish tint which reduced the candlepower, a situation which had caused the British to abandon this system. Reflector shape was not uniform; many were not parabolic but spherical and were too thin and/or badly bent from repeated cleaning. However, the Lewis system was cost effective versus the Fresnel lens, so its use continued for roughly twenty years before the final switch.

By the late 1830s, the U. S. maritime community urged the government to adopt the Fresnel lens. In 1838 Congress sent Commodore Matthew Perry to Europe to purchase two of the lenses: one first-order fixed and one second-order flashing. These lenses were installed in the twin lights in Navesink, New Jersey and produced a light far superior to any other. Some 12 years later, when in need of repair, these lights were still noted to be of significantly better quality than nearby Sandy Hook which was equipped with the Lewis system. By the time of the Civil War, all lighthouses were fitted with Fresnel lenses and most had new lanterns. The largest lenses (first through third order) were considered suitable for coastal lights, with the smaller three orders installed in harbor or bay lights. A middle lens, 3.5 order, was developed later and used primarily in the Great Lakes lights.

Oil from the head of the sperm whale was the first fuel source for lens lamps in America's lighthouses. But, with a dramatic increase in the price of sperm oil between 1840 and early 1850s, another fuel source was sought. England and France were using colza, an oil made from rapeseed. The Lighthouse Board hoped that farmers would take note and begin to grow this plant, but they did not respond. Other options then had to be determined: lard oil was used for a time replaced later by kerosene about 1870. Although effective, the kerosene was extremely volatile and required careful handling. Typically a small, brick or stone building provided safe storage for the volatile oil. At the turn of the century, the incandescent oil vapor lamp came into use. Giving off a bright light, this lamp was used until electricity reached individual lighthouses--in some cases not until after World War II. The first light lit with electricity was the Statue of Liberty in 1886 which served as a "lighthouse" until 1903.

The 19th century also saw introduction of new materials and designs used in U.S. lighthouse construction. Cast iron structures became popular and a design using iron and wood in combination created pile lighthouses. The development of screwpile structures was particularly valuable as they could be built in the water on top of or near the navigational hazzard. A variation on the pile lighthouse, in which the iron piles, or legs, were driven into the sea bottom or set into rocks, was developed in the mid 1800s. The first pile lighthouse in the U.S. was constructed at Minots Ledge and went into service in 1850 but was blown over by a storm in 1852. Screwpile structures were built in the United States along the Chesapeake Bay, North Carolina sounds and the Gulf Coast. Each lighthouse had nine legs, one in the center with eight surrounding it in an octagonal arrangement; a platform was then built on top of the legs. The lighthouse, constructed on the flat surface, was a one-story dwelling for living quarters with lantern room and light on top.

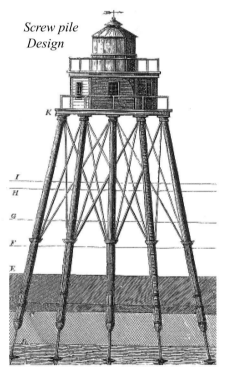

Screw pile Design

In the late 1800s Caisson lighthouses, with concrete bases positioned securely on the sea bottom, were used extensively in the United States, particularly along the northern and mid-Atlantic coasts. Although the term "caisson" technically refers only to the bottom of the cylinder, typically the definition includes the entire cylindrical tube which is the foundation of the lighthouse. Because these sturdy structures readily withstood severe weather and bumps from passing vessels, they replaced lightships stationed at sites that were too rough for bay screwpile or harbor lights.

Seven coastal tall towers were built during the 1850s (including those at Fire Island and Cape Hatteras), then another five in the 1870s and three in the 1880s. These structures, like earlier comparable structures, were made of brick. Often the US coastal lights were also painted with daymarks to differentiate them during daylight hours; most of these are seen along the Atlantic coast. Patterns are duplicated, but lights with identical markings are widely separated. By the turn of the century, an extensive system of navigational aids was in place along the US coasts, with the 1920s the heyday of lighthouses.

Regulation & Administration

In 1851 Congress authorized a board to investigate the state of the country's navigational aids. The findings indicated that significant problems existed, among them poor management, towers too short for proper range, improper reflector shape, and poorly trained-to-incompetent keepers. The investigatory board noted a "better system" clearly was needed and recommended creation of a Lighthouse Board to manage the nation's lighthouses and other aids to navigation. Additionally, the plan called for establishment of lighthouse districts and installation of a Fresnel lens in all existing and new lighthouses. In 1852 the Lighthouse Board was officially established by Congress although it had commenced work well before that time.

The Board divided the country into twelve districts: two in the Great Lakes, seven along the Atlantic coast, two in the Gulf of Mexico and one for the West coast. As both the system and country grew, additional districts were added, finally totalling eighteen. An inspector managed each district; local customs collectors functioned as assistants, who typically hired and paid the keepers, and handled a variety of administrative duties. Gradually these assistants were phased out and the Lighthouse Board assigned an army engineer to each district. The district then had a naval officer (inspector) to ensure the lighthouses worked properly and that the keepers performed duties as required; the engineer (army officer) was responsible for construction, repair and maintenance .

Having brought order and improvement to the nation's aids to navigation, the Lighthouse Board was replaced in 1910 by the Lighthouse Bureau (or Lighthouse Service) as governing body. Congress enacted the change in order to instate civilian control of lighthouse matters. This organization was merged into the Coast Guard in 1939 and all individuals were given the choice of remaining civilian employees or joining the Coast Guard. By the mid 1900s advances in technology had created a sophisticated system to warn and guide mariners. The lightkeeper was gradually replaced by automated equipment and many lights abandoned altogether. In the 1960s the process of automation of all US lighthouses was undertaken; today only Boston Harbor light is staffed and will remain so to commemorate the historic significance of lighthouses and light keepers in maritime history.

Changing Roles: Looking Forward

Today the lighthouse represents a symbol of maritime tradition and cultural history. With automation now standard and navigational technology often eliminating the need for particular lights entirely, other roles are being created for many of these locations, saving them from destruction, neglect and ruin. No longer simply left to fall victim to vandalism and the elements, lights which are no longer active navigational aids have taken on another important function. Local groups are restoring lighthouses in their area for use as tourist sites and interpretive centers so that future generations can learn about and, to some extent, relive a past era. Extensive preservation and reconstruction efforts are underway nationwide to return lighthouses to their former condition; those threatened by erosison are being relocated rather than being left to fall into the sea. The Maine Lights Program, an innovative program completed in 1998, saved numerous lighthouses and stations by assigning stewardship to local communities, private non-profit organizations, or appropriate State or Federal agencies. School children, visitors and local residents are now afforded access to many lighthouses nationwide and are then able to better appreciate the history they represent.

The few remaining lightkeepers (only at Boston Light in the U.S. and several throughout the Canadian provinces) also find their duties changing in light of continuing advances in technology. Time formerly spent polishing lenses, winding clockwork mechanisms and rescuing shipwreck victims is now used to interpret for visitors the spirit and history of the lightkeeping tradition. The changing role for lighthouses and the new "lightkeeper" ensures that the history represented by both will not fade.

Maine's Lighthouse Heritage

Following the American Revolution individual states retained control of lighthouses in their territories; at that time, Maine was a district of Massachusetts. In 1787, responding to petitions from citizens of Portland and Casco Bay, the Massachusetts legislature appropriated funds for a lighthouse at Portland Head. Construction was halted however when funds ran out just short of completion. When the US Lighthouse Service was established in 1789, the Federal government assumed responsibility for all lighthouses and aids to navigation and Congress promptly appropriated an additional $1500 for completion of Portland Head Light. First lit in January 1791, President George Washington appointed the first keeper, Joseph Greenleaf.

Maritime commerce in Maine increased rapidly in the late 18th and early 19th centuries. Between 1791 and 1820, seven additional lighthouses were built along the portion of the Massachusetts coast which would become Maine: Seguin Island (1795), Franklin Island (1805), Whitehead Island (1807), Wood Island (1808), West Quoddy Head (1808), Boon Island (1811) and Petit Manan Island (1817). Six of these were primary or second-ary seacoast lights, providing a coasting vessel headed Downeast from Kittery to Penobscot Bay with at least one lighthouse in view at all times. Further north however only two beacons (Petit Manan and West Quoddy Head) were in place to guide the mariner. With statehood in 1820, Maine gained representation in Washington and a local Superintendent of Lighthouses based in Portland. A boom in lighthouse construction accompanied growth in population in the new state and a flourishing maritime trade; 17 new lights were built along the Maine coast during the next 15 years, predominantly of rubble stone (local granite). By 1852, thirty four lighthouses along the Maine coast made it possible to sail from Kittery to West Quoddy with two or more beacons visible at all times. Many prominent harbors, bays and significant hazzards also were marked.

West Quoddy Head Light

Coincident with formation of the Lighthouse Board in 1852, Maine enjoyed a second boom in lighthouse construction. During the next 10 years, 14 new structures were built and 16 extensively upgraded or rebuilt with installation of Fresnel lenses in all Maine lighthouses accomplished by 1860. Two additional periods of rapid expansion occurred: during the 1870s (12 structures newly built or extensively remodeled) and during the 20-year period 1890 to 1910. Whitlock's Mill Light on the St. Croix River is Maine's most "recent" lighthouse, com-pleted in 1919. By the early 1930s changes in patterns of commerce and shipping activity along the Maine coast, coupled with advances in technology, prompted a move to decommission a number of manned lightstations, replacing them with unattended acetylene lights, turned on and off by a light-sensitive mechanism. Eight lights were replaced, six sold to private ownership and two ceded to local towns. Five of the six privately-owned sites still exist as summer homes; Crabtree Ledge light was destroyed by a winter storm. In 1939, the US Lighthouse Service dissolved and the Coast Guard assumed responsibility for aids to navigation. By the mid 1960s, all civilian keepers in Maine had retired (the last one was at Squirrel Point Light on the Kennebec River). The remaining lighthouse keepers in Maine were Coast Guard military personnel.

The increased cost of manned lighthouses at remote offshore locations and rapid progress in automation tech-nology, led the Coast Guard to initiate removal of keepers from all US lighthouses; by 1978 there were only 22 manned lighthouses remaining in Maine. This program was completed in 1990 when the keeper at Goat Island Light (off Kennebunkport) was withdrawn. An effort was then undertaken to further reduce maintenance costs at lightstations by demolishing redundant structures, resulting in the loss of numerous keeper's houses and other outbuildings. This policy was soon met with significant public outcry; many of Maine's light stations were subsequently placed on the National Register. The Coast Guard gradually realized that adaptive reuse of these structures was preferable to destruction. Some keeper's quarters now serve as housing for Coast Guard personnel (Bass Harbor, Portland Head, West Quoddy Head, Kennebec River Range); others have been converted to museums, one is a bed and breakfast. The Maine Lights Program was a key initiative which successfully placed additional locations in the hands of local communities, nonprofit organizations and individuals with the stipula-tion that public access be afforded and careful preservation accomplished.

The Maine Lighthouse Style

The words "Maine" and "lighthouse" are now often synonymous as the wide variety in appearance, construction, architectural style, location and individual histories makes the lighthouses of Maine particularly appealing. In addition to lights which mark important harbors and bays, the Maine coast has a number of both primary and secondary seacoast beacons and one "set" of range lights (Kennebec River). Today all active lighthouses in Maine are automated and unattended; various structures at many stations have been intentionally demolished or destroyed by storm or vandalism. However, recent preservation efforts have enabled reconstruction at many locations and preservation of existing buildings at others so that an appreciation of each lighthouse's "character" is possible.

Early Maine lighthouses were constructed primarily of rubble stone (natural granite stones mortared together) usually around a brick core. Typically these towers were 20 to 30 feet tall; solid walls three to four feet thick at the base, tapered to approximately two feet at the top. The towers were topped with a cast-iron lantern room with octagonal sections bolted together. Surviving examples of such construction are Pemaquid Point, Owls Head, Dyce Head lights. Some early keeper's houses also were of rubble stone construction, but none have survived. All early structures stressed function and simplicity with few, if any, nonfunctional adornments. Local contractors worked with a minimum of drawings and detailed specifications, with much discretion left to a local supervisor (prior to 1847 the local Collector of Customs). The quality of construction work was directly dependent on the experience and diligence of this supervisor, varying from excellent to shoddy. Extensive repairs, including eventual replacement of the lighthouse tower, often were required.

As lighthouse construction progessed along the Maine coast, dressed granite and masonry towers predominated, producing more secure structures in exposed locations (Monhegan Is., Saddleback Ledge, Mt. Desert Rock, Boon & Petit Manan Is.). The proportion of the tower varied from short and squat (Saddleback), to more evenly balanced structures (Monhegan, Whitehead Is.), to the tall slender towers of Boon and Petit Manan Islands. During Maine's 1850s building boom, a number of the minor, less exposed towers were brick and again reflected a simple, functional design (Browns Head, Bass Harbor Head). The keeper's quarters typically were 1-1/2 story Cape Cod style cottages, often with a covered walkway attached to the lighthouse tower to afford protection from severe winter weather and to facilitate carrying oil, heated on the kitchen stove, to the lantern room.

Early Monhegan Light

In the 1870s cast iron gave lighthouse designers increased options to approach the requirements of functionality, durability and strength; aesthetics became an element and "architectural statements" were made (Portland Breakwater, Cape Neddick, Cape Elizabeth). Keeper's houses also moved to larger, more elaborate designs: 2-1/2 stories, porches, Queen Anne style adornments (Marshall Point, Isle au Haut). In the late 1800s, Maine added four additional cast iron, caisson-style lighthouses often referred to as "spark plug lights" (Lubec Channel, Spring Point Ledge, Goose Rocks, Crabtree Ledge). These structures also boasted ornamentation around the windows and doors, ornamental brackets and finials. A series of small wooden lighthouses built in 1898 along the Kennebec River was the last group of a distinct type of structure built in Maine (Doubling Point, Squirrel Point, Perkins Is., Kennebec Ranges).

The typical light station was not unlike a small, rural homestead with barn, storage sheds and privy; farm animals were raised and vegetable gardens tended when the location permitted. A boathouse provided storage for the keeper's primary mode of transport to the nearest town either from an island or mainland light with no overland access. Small brick oil houses were built to store the extremely volatile kerosene. Many of these structures remain today. Most of the covered walkways have been removed. Visitors were encouraged to drop in at the accessible lightstations and keepers encouraged to be gracious hosts, showing off the spectacular coastal settings and impressive living quarters. Even the remote offshore station at Saddleback Ledge welcomed visitors and became "tourist" destination. The Lighthouse Establishment understood the value of good public relations to be gained by the "open door" policy. Through expanding and ongoing efforts to restore, preserve and open additional lighthouses to visitors, the farsighted approach taken by the Lighthouse Establishment is underscored and appreciated.

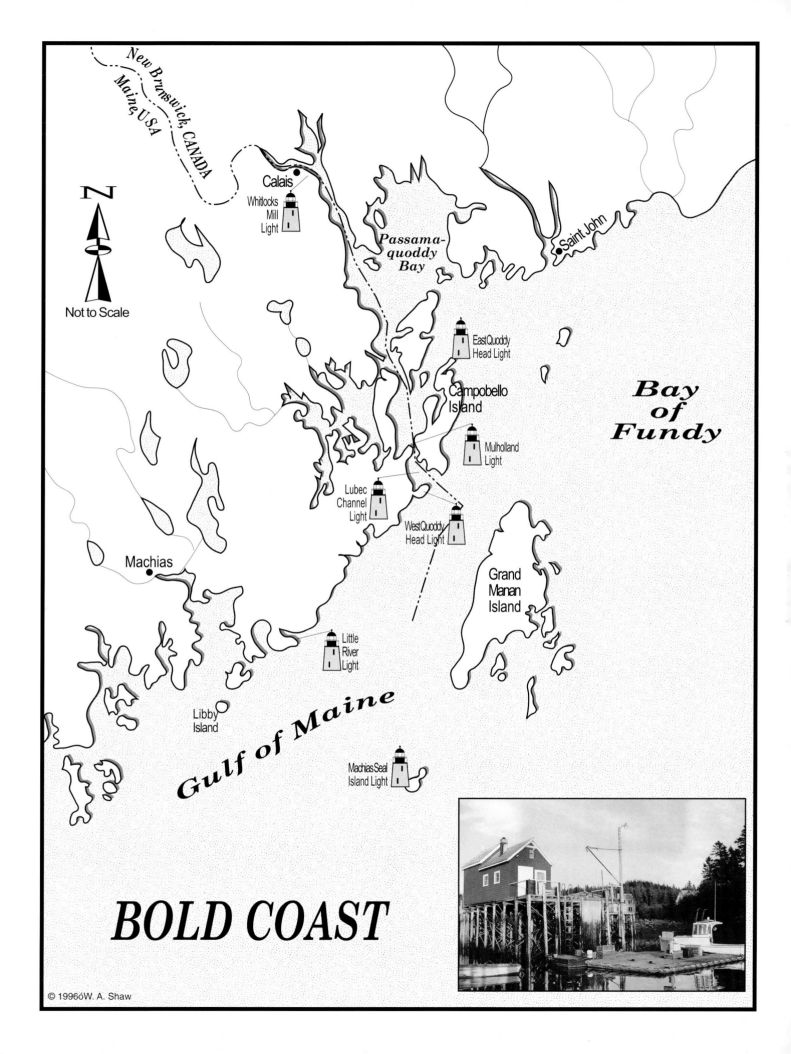

New Brunswick, CANADA
Maine USA

N

Not to Scale

Calais

Whitlocks
Mill
Light

Passama-
quoddy
Bay

Saint John

East Quoddy
Head Light

Campobello
Island

Bay
of
Fundy

Mulholland
Light

Lubec
Channel
Light

West Quoddy
Head Light

Machias

Grand
Manan
Island

Little
River
Light

Libby
Island

Gulf of Maine

Machias Seal
Island Light

BOLD COAST

East Quoddy Head Light

Located on the northern end of Campobello Island, New Brunswick, the light is maintained by the Canadian Coast Guard. The large red cross is typical of Canadian lights.

Alexander Findlay in 1867 wrote that "the lighthouses of New Brunswick and Nova Scotia, where necessary, are painted with black or red stripes to distinguish the towers from the land." He continues, "after the snow is gone off the land, the accumulations against the fences, which generally run at right angles to the coast, and which continue for some time after it (the snow) has disappeared from the fields themselves, have exactly the appearance of a white tower." The light is also known as Head Harbour Light.

An organization has recently formed to undertake restoration and repair of the station, including possible construction of bridges to aid in public access to the grounds.

*Summer home of Franklin Roosevelt, Campobello Island, NB
en route to East Quoddy Head Lighthouse*

Directions: Cross into Canada at Lubec, Maine and continue approximately 2.5 miles past the customs station and Roosevelt Park. Turn right at a"Y" intersection, NB 774North. Continue on this road for about seven miles through Wilson's Beach to Head Harbour and the light. The road (Lighthouse Rd) becomes a dirt road shortly before ending at the parking area.

There are trails around the area, including series of iron rail stairways which make the light accessible directly at low tide only. A sign warns of rapidly changing tides and weather conditions; there is about a two-hour period to cross and return from the light without being stranded on the island for six to eight hours.

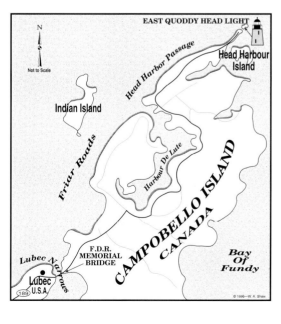

Mulholland Light

On the east side of Lubec Channel on Campobello Island, the light is easily seen from the Maine side of the channel and is easily accessible from the Canadian side; good views also are possible from the bridge connecting Lubec, Maine to Campobello Island, New Brunswick. The lighthouse is part of the Roosevelt Campobello International Park and picnic grounds. Mulholland is not a functioning light.

Directions: Cross over to New Brunswick, Canada at Lubec, Maine, taking the first left after the customs station, just opposite the welcome/information center. The road leads down a hill, then bears right; a small park and the light are just to the left. No stopping on the bridge is permitted.

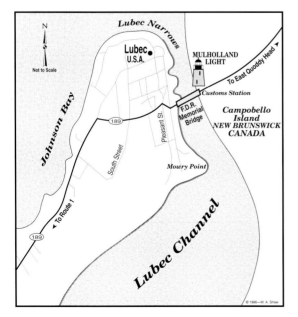

"Mulholland Point Lighthouse
Erected 1885
Donated to
Roosevelt Campobello International Park
December 4, 1985"

Whitlocks Mill Light

The present Whitlocks Mill Light is the northernmost light in the United States and one of Maine's youngest lighthouses. In 1892 a lantern was displayed from a tree on the American side of the St.Croix River near Calais. The city was an important lumber port and construction of a more permanent lighthouse was undertaken in 1910. The new tower received a fourth-order Fresnel lens. The present keeper's house also was built in 1910.

The lighthouse was automated in 1969 and the lens removed. In the 1970s the station was leased to the Washington County Vocational Technical Institute. The grounds are now privately owned.

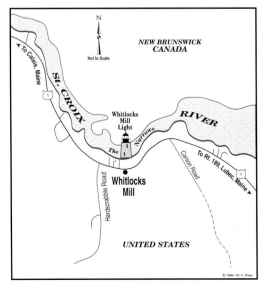

Directions: The light can be located by taking U.S. Route 1 from Whiting, through Red Beach to the Taylor Furniture Store, just south of Calais. **Turn around** and count four driveways **back on the left** from the store (to the south). A narrow, dirt road leads to the light and private residence; the area is not a public park. The light also can be seen in the distance from a roadside park area off Route 1, about five miles north from the entrance to the St. Croix Island International Historic Site.

Lubec Channel Light

In the late 19th century Lubec was an important trade and fishing port. Lubec Channel Light was built at the harbor's western entrance in 1889, a typical "sparkplug" style cast-iron structure of the period. A fifth-order Fresnel lens was installed and initially miniature brass lighthouses topped each baluster on the lighthouse gallery. There were five levels in the tower, two of which were living quarters for the keepers. This location was a stag station, staffed by two male keepers.

The light was automated in 1939 and in 1968 a modern optic replaced the Fresnel lens. Discontinuation of the light was planned for 1989, but local residents mounted a "Save the Sparkplug" campaign. In 1992 a $700,000 renovation restored Lubec Channel Light. The lighthouse can be seen easily from several points on shore.

Directions: Turn off U.S. Route 1 at Whiting, onto ME 189 to Lubec.
Continue about four miles, then turn right onto South Lubec/Boot Cove Road (marked with a "Quoddy Head State Park" sign). The Lubec Channel light can be seen to the left at about 1/3 to 1/2 mile; it can also be seen from ME 189 crossing into Canada. Additionally, there are tour boats out of Lubec which afford closer views of this light.

23

West Quoddy Head Light

Located on the easternmost point in the continental United States, the red and white striped lighthouse marks the southwest entrance to Quoddy Channel. In 1806 a group of concerned citizens chose West Quoddy Head as a suitable place for a lighthouse to aid mariners coming into the west entrance to Quoddy Roads between the mainland and Campobello Island. The first rubblestone lighthouse was built there two years later by order of Thomas Jefferson. West Quoddy Head light received one of the nation's first fog bells in 1820. The keeper was required to strike the bell by hand in foggy weather, a frequent occurrence in the nearby Bay of Fundy. For his trouble, Congress in 1827 alotted the keeper an additional $60 annually.

The lighthouse may have been rebuilt in 1853, but was not long standing; the present 49-foot brick tower was erected in 1858 and a third-order Fresnel lens was installed. A 1-1/2 story Victorian keeper's house was built in that same year; in 1869 a trumpet fog whistle replaced the earlier bells.

The light was automated in 1988 and is now part of Quoddy Head State Park; grounds are open to the public with trails along the shore and to the lighthouse. The "west" in West Quoddy Head, refers to its location west of East Quoddy Head in nearby New Brunswick, Canada.

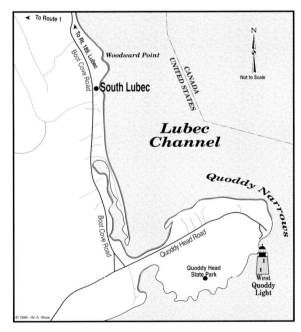

Directions: From U.S. Route 1 at Whiting, Maine turn onto ME 189 and continue for about four miles. Turn right onto South Lubec/Boot Cove Road (marked with a "Quoddy Head State Park" sign) and continue to a fork in the road, again marked with "Quoddy Head State Park". Bear left and continue on to the park and light station. At the entrance to the station turn right onto the road leading to the parking area. A short trail to the left leads to the light; other trails to the right offer views of the light, cliffs and islands.

Twelve miles off the coast from Cutler, Maine, this light station is maintained by the Canadian government although it is in waters claimed both by the United States and Canada. Canadian lightkeepers man the station due to a question of sovereignty, with both Canada and the United States claiming the island and surrounding waters. The island is home to a large puffin colony and other sea birds, carefully protected by the Canadian Wildlife Service. Charter trips to view the light and the puffins are available from Grand Manan Island in New Brunswick(Canada) as well as Jonesport and Cutler, Maine.

Machias Seal Island Light

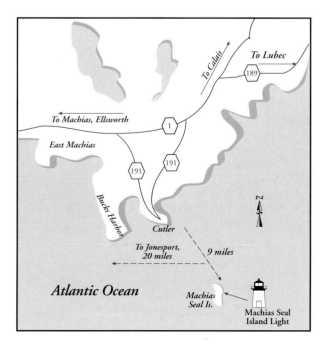

Little River Light

In 1847, as the trade, shipbuilding and fishing industries grew in Cutler Harbor, a lighthouse was built on Little River Island at the harbor entrance. The light also was intended as an intermediate mark between West Quoddy Head to the north and Machias Seal Island to the southeast. A stone keeper's house and stone tower were erected and fifth-order Fresnel lens installed in 1855. The lighthouse was rebuilt in 1876; the 41-foot cast-iron tower still stands. A wood-framed Victorian keeper's house replaced the initial dwelling in 1888. Little River Island is near the mainland, so the station was a much sought-after assignment offering spectacular views of the Bay of Fundy. Cutler became an important coastal defense site in 1960 when two 1000-

foot communications towers were erected at the town's naval base. The towers provide communications with the Navy submarine fleet in the North Atlantic, Europe and Arctic.

Little River Light was automated in 1975 and in 1980 the Fresnel lens was removed. A skeleton tower is now the functioning light. The oil house, keeper's house and boat house still remain on the island. In 2000 the American Lighthouse Foundation assumed responsibility for the restoration and preservation of the station. The lighthouse is on the seaward side of the island and cannot be seen from the mainland but must be viewed from the water.

Directions: From U.S. Route 1 at East Machias, turn south onto RT 191. Follow that road into Cutler Harbor where charter arrangements may be made. Trips from Cutler to Machias Seal Island will pass this light on return.

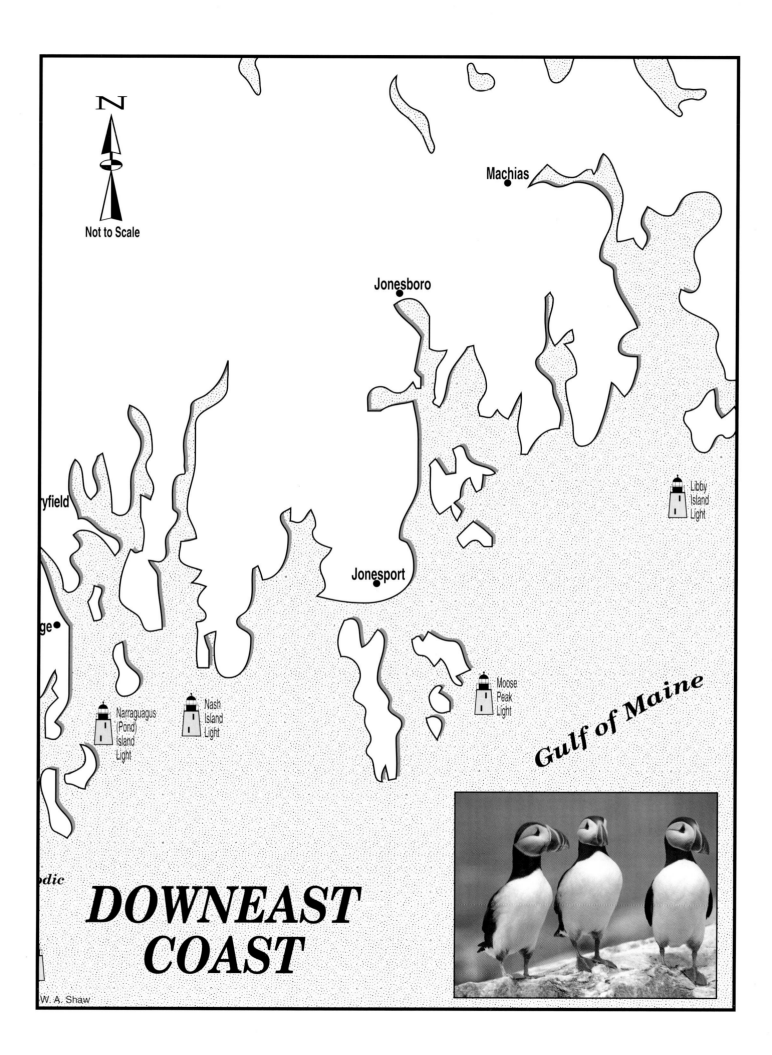

N

Not to Scale

Machias

Jonesboro

Libby
Island
Light

yfield

Jonesport

ge

Moose
Peak
Light

Narraguagus
(Pond)
Island
Light

Nash
Island
Light

Gulf of Maine

odic

DOWNEAST COAST

W. A. Shaw

Libby Island Light

At the east entrance to Machias Bay, scene of the first naval battle of the American Revolution, Libby Island Light is the easternmost lighthouse in the United States and was known for many years as Machias Light. The 120-acre island is actually two islands connected by a sandbar.

The present 42-foot granite tower was built at the southern tip of Libby Island in 1824, along with a 1-1/2 story wood frame keeper's house; a Fresnel lens was installed in 1855. Because the island is among the foggiest locations along the Maine coast, a fog horn was installed in 1884. This addition required an assistant keeper. Two new dwellings were built to accommodate the keepers and familes and by the early 1900s as many as 20 people were living on the island. Notable among vessels wrecked in the area was the schooner *Caledonia*, in 1878, out of Nova Scotia.

In 1974 the Fresnel lens was removed when the lighthouse was automated; the light was recently converted to solar power. All buildings except the lighthouse and one outbuilding have been destroyed. The light must be viewed by boat.

Moose Peak Light

A lighthouse on the east point of Mistake Island, about five miles south of Jonesport, was authorized by President John Quincy Adams in 1825. The first light was completed in 1827 and fitted with a second-order Fresnel lens in 1856. The present 57 foot brick tower was built in 1887. In 1901 the original keeper's house was replaced and connected to the lighthouse by a walkway.

Moose Peak Light was the the foggiest station on the Maine Coast. A fog signal was installed in 1912 and,during the period from 1918 to 1934, the keepers recorded that the island averaged 1,607 hours of fog per year, or about 20% of the time.

The light was automated in 1972 and the Fresnel lens removed. In 1982 the keeper's house was blown up by a team of Green Berets as a training exercise. The exercise also damaged panes in the lighthouse lantern. Although in clear weather the light can be seen distantly from Great Wass Island, it is best viewed by boat or air.

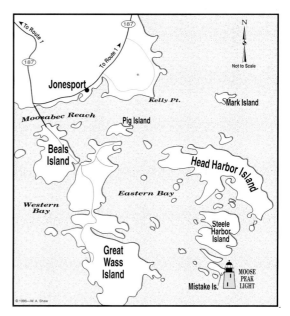

Directions: In Jonesport at the "Bridge Street" and " Beal's Island" signs turn off ME 187 onto the bridge to Beal's Island. On the island, turn left and continue on Great Wass Road across Beal's Island to the road's end on Great Wass Island. Walk to the top of the rocky knoll or walk along the shore to the point; Moose Peak light can be seen in the distance, to the east, in the V-shaped part of the island.

Petit Manan Light

Established in 1817 and rebuilt of granite in 1855, this is the second tallest lighthouse in Maine, standing 123 feet above mean high water (the tower is 119 feet high). The light is located on the east point of Petit Manan Island, 2.5 miles off Petit Manan Point in South Milbridge. The station also has a fog signal to warn of a nearby reef as the location is one of the foggiest along the East Coast, engulfed in fog about 20% of the year. The island was named by explorer Samuel de Champlain because it reminded him of Grand Manan to the northeast. The "Manan" comes from the Micmac Indian word for "island out to sea".

The process of rebuilding the light in 1855 was twofold. The granite was first cut and assembled at a quarry in Trenton, Maine. Numbered stones were dismantled and brought to the island by boat for reassembly. Constantly buffeted by storms, the tower was strengthened by addition of iron tie rods in 1887. The lantern room at one time held a second-order Fresnel lens. That lens is now displayed at the Shore Village Museum in Rockland, Maine.

After automation of the light, the island was turned over to the U.S. Fish and Wildlife Service as a wildlife refuge. The island now supports common, arctic and roseate tern colonies, a breeding colony of Atlantic puffins and common eiders. Fish and Wildlife staff use the tower as an observation post and live in the keeper's house.

Puffin watches from Bar Harbor go to Petit Manan and spend time offshore watching the birds. The lighthouse can also be seen in the distance from Petit Manan Point in Petit Manan National Wildlife Refuge.

Directions: On U.S. Route 1, between Steuben and Milbridge, turn south onto Pigeon Hill Rd (marked). The turn is approximately three miles **west** of the intersection of US 1 and US 1A in Milbridge and three miles **east** of the Unionville & Steuben Rd. intersection. Continue on Pigeon Hill Rd. to the Chitman Point area (approximately 5.5-6.0 miles) to the fisherman's coop. Petit Manan can be seen in the distance. Continuing further south about 0.5 mile brings you to the Petit Manan National Wildlife Refuge . There is a parking lot straight ahead; just south of the parking lot is the beginning of a five-mile Shore Trail. The first two miles of the trail lead to the eastern side of Petit Manan Point peninsula and good, distant views of the light.

Nash Island Light

Built to mark the entrance to Moose-a-Bec Reach, Pleasant Bay and Harrington Bay near South Addison, the first lighthouse on Nash Island was authorized in 1837 and completed in 1838. A Fresnel lens was added in 1856. The original round tower was rebuilt in 1873 and the 51-foot square brick structure still stands. A fog bell was added in 1887. This station was one of the few where children of lighthouse keepers attended school on the island for the earlier grades.

In 1958 the lighthouse was automated; the keeper's dwellings, oil house and all outbuildings were destroyed, leaving only the tower remaining. Remains of the foundation(s) are still visible. The light was discontinued in 1982 and replaced by an offshore buoy.

The island is now a Fish and Wildlife refuge for ducks and nesting birds; a flock of nearly 100 sheep also inhabits the island. The owner of the sheep is Genevieve "Jenny" Crione, now a resident of South Addison, and daughter of a former lighthouse keeper. Past 90, she still goes lobstering and makes occasional trips to the island to check her flock.

A group of concerned citizens organized a successful effort to gain custodianship of the lighthouse and to undertake restoration and renovation. Within the past two years the exterior has been restored and repainted; tower window panes also have been replaced. The light can be seen distantly from points along the shore in South Addison but is best viewed by boat (**Note map page 35**).

Narraguagus (Pond) Island Light

Called Pond Island Light by people in the area, the lighthouse is located southeast of Milbridge, Maine on a rock ledge on the seaward side of Pond Island in Narraguagus Bay. In 1853 President Franklin Pierce authorized construction of the lighthouse to mark the entrance to Millbridge Harbor. Initially the light was located on top of the keeper's dwelling. Three acres later were purchased from an island farmer for the light station buildings. In 1875 a new house was built and much of the original house removed from around the tower.

A luxury inn and clubhouse were built on the island in 1878, with a golf course added in 1920. The posh resort gradually declined but the large common building remains and is used by island summer residents. Narraguagus light was discontinued in 1934; the lighthouse, outbuildings and surrounding five acres were sold at auction. The lighthouse and property are still privately owned and must be viewed by boat.

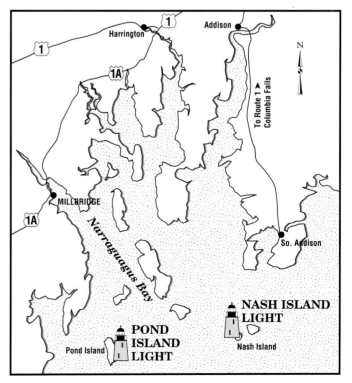

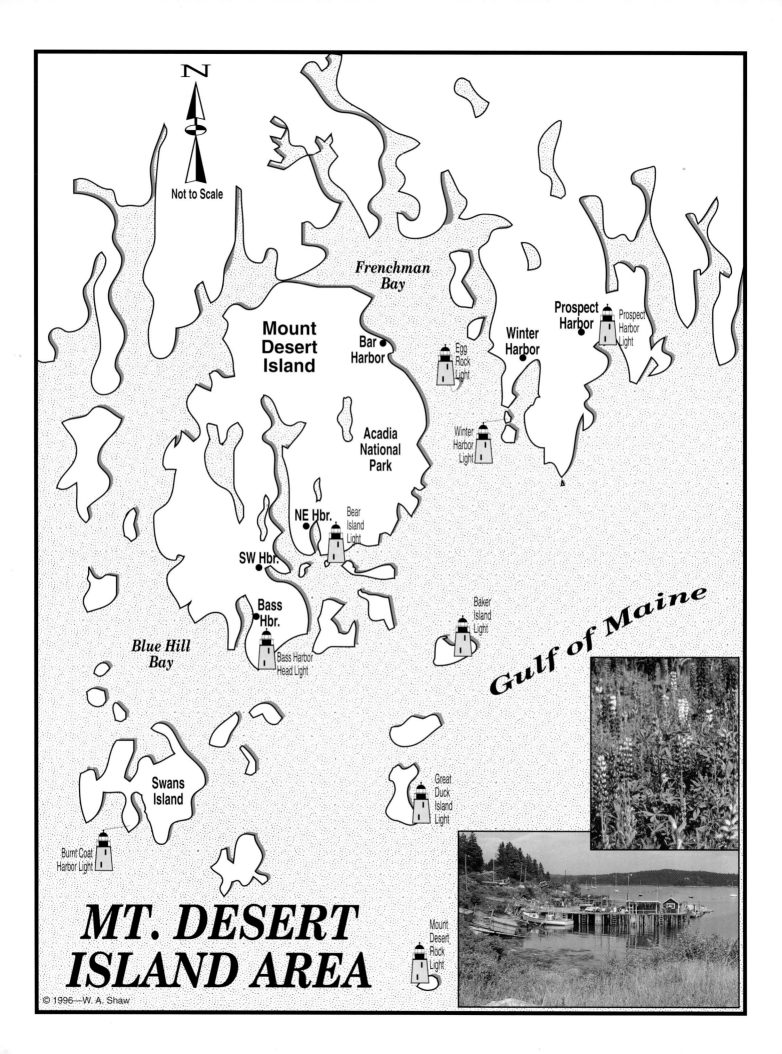

N

Not to Scale

Frenchman Bay

Mount Desert Island

Bar Harbor

Egg Rock Light

Winter Harbor

Prospect Harbor

Prospect Harbor Light

Acadia National Park

Winter Harbor Light

NE Hbr.

Bear Island Light

SW Hbr.

Blue Hill Bay

Bass Hbr.

Baker Island Light

Gulf of Maine

Bass Harbor Head Light

Swans Island

Great Duck Island Light

Burnt Coat Harbor Light

MT. DESERT ISLAND AREA

Mount Desert Rock Light

Baker Island Light

Baker island, at the southwest entrance to Frenchman Bay, is located about four miles from Mt. Desert Island and is one of five islands that make up the Cranberry Isles. President John Quincy Adams authorized construction of a lighthouse on the island in 1828 in order to mark the western approach to Frenchman Bay, dangerous ledges and shoals around the Cranberry Isles. The wood tower, built on the highest point on the island, was the earliest lighthouse in the Mt. Desert area.

William and Hanna Gilley took possession of Baker Island in the early 19th century. Gilley was appointed first keeper and held the position for 21 years until his dismissal in 1846; he then moved to Great Duck Island. Two Gilley sons subsequently harassed the new lighthouse keeper, prompting eviction efforts by the government. The Gilleys resisted and legal battles ensued for years; the lighthouse station eventually became government property with the Gilleys retaining the remainder of the island.

The present 43-foot brick tower was built in 1855 and a fourth-order Fresnel lens installed. There was at one time a short covered passageway between the dwelling and lighthouse. The light was automated and converted to solar power in 1966. In 1989 the Maine Historic Preservation Commission refurbished the light but in 1991 the Coast Guard announced plans to deactivate the light, allowing that trees obscured a clear view of the beacon. Complaints from local mariners convinced the Coast Guard to reconsider and the trees were trimmed a bit.

Plans for discontinuation of Baker Island Light were renewed in 1997. Local mariners and others again convinced the Coast Guard the light was needed but the problem with the trees remains an issue. The 123-acre wooded island is now part of Acadia National Park which offers summer excursions to the island from Northeast Harbor.

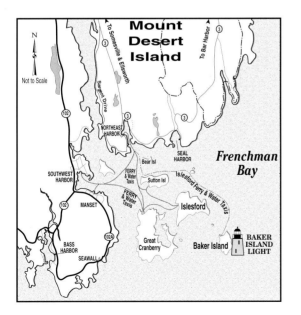

Directions: From ME 3 or 233 (Eagle Lake Road) in Mt. Desert, take ME 198 south to Northeast Harbor. Turn left off ME 198 in Northeast Harbor at Harbor Drive (sign indicates "marina"). The *Islesford Ferry,* docked at Northeast Harbor Marina, offers trips to the island. A naturalist (sponsored by Acadia National Park) accompanies visitors and leads a walk which includes a visit to the lighthouse. Also by custom charter.

Winter Harbor (Mark Island) Light

Winter Harbor was long a favorite safe harbor for mariners seeking shelter from storms. In 1856 a lighthouse was built on nearby Mark Island to guide vessels into the harbor and to warn of dangerous ledges nearby.

The light was discontinued in 1934 and replaced by a lighted buoy to the southeast. Subsequently the property was sold to a variety of individuals. The current owner has undertaken careful renovation of the keeper's house, outbuildings and lighthouse; his work is ongoing.

Various points along the loop road in the Schoodic Peninsula section of Acadia National Park offer distant offshore views. Some excursion boats from Bar Harbor offer closer views from the water.

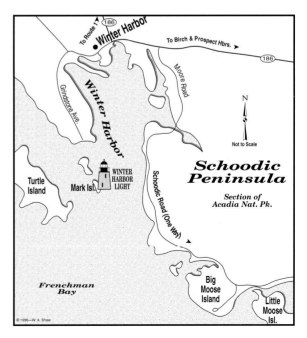

Directions: From U.S. Route 1, turn south onto ME 186 at West Gouldsboro, toward Schoodic Point. Turn off ME 186 at the marked road leading to Acadia National Park, Schoodic Peninsula (between Birch Harbor and Winter Harbor). The park's perimeter road is a one-way loop and the lighthouse/island can be seen from that road. Excursion and tour boats from Bar Harbor offer closer views for better photography.

Prospect Harbor Light

The small town of Prospect Harbor boasted a large fishing fleet in the 19th century, prompting construction of a lighthouse in 1850 to mark the east side of the inner harbor entrance. Deactivated in 1859, the light was reactivated by the Lighthouse Board in 1870. The initial granite lighthouse attached to a keeper's house was replaced in 1891 with the present 38-foot wood-framed lighthouse and new 1-1/2 story dwelling. The lantern held a fifth-order Fresnel lens; a stone oil house was added in 1905.

In 1934 the keeper was removed from Prospect Harbor light and the Fresnel lens removed in 1951, replaced by an automatic modern optic. The lighthouse is now on the grounds of a Navy Special Operations Command installation.

The light may be easily seen from across the harbor and may also be photographed from just outside the base entrance. Walking along the rocks at the water's edge affords excellent views; there is a scheduled open house each spring.

Directions: From U.S. Route 1, take either ME 186 or 195 to Prospect Harbor. Turn at the sign to Corea at the intersection of these two routes. FR 605 (Lighthouse Point Road) is about 0.2 mile—ME 195 bears left to Corea, but continue straight on FR 605 to the restricted U.S. Navy communications station. The light is easily photographed from the shoreline. Alternatively, across the harbor the light can be seen and photographed from the grounds of the Stinson Canning Company (on ME 186 entering Prospect Harbor) or from a turnout on the shoulder of ME 186, just north of the canning company.

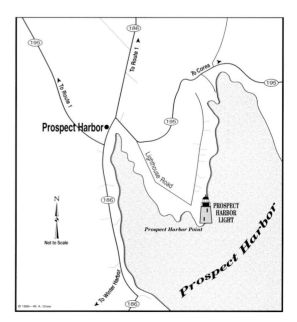

Egg Rock Light

Built on a rocky ledge in 1875, this light was intended to mark the entrance to Frenchman Bay. Egg Rock Light consists of a brick tower in the center of a 1-1/2 story wood keeper's house; the design was intended to conserve space. The lighthouse originally held a fifth-order Fresnel lens. In 1876 the building was damaged by a March gale which moved the bell tower 30 feet. Following similar damage in an 1887 blizzard, a new skeletal bell tower was constructed and later replaced by a steam-driven fog horn.

In 1902 Egg Rock Light was upgraded with installation of a new fourth-order lens; the characteristic was changed from fixed red to flashing white. The grounding of the battleship Massachusetts in 1903 prompted addition of a new fog horn to the station in 1904. However, Joseph Pulitzer, who owned a nearby estate, protested that noise from the new horn disturbed his quietude; the signal then was turned to face away from his property and remains so directed.

The light was automated and Coast Guard keepers removed in 1976. Rotating aerobeacons were installed following removal of the lighthouse lantern. This change gave Egg Rock Light a decidedly homely appearance; it was labeled by many as the least attractive lighthouse in Maine.

In 1986, responding to complaints, the Coast Guard installed a new aluminum lantern, 190mm optic and railing around the lantern deck perimeter to improve the appearance of the lighthouse. A boathouse, oil house and generator house still remain on the property.

Almost all excursion boats from Bar Harbor pass this lighthouse each day as do whale watches leaving the harbor. The light may also be seen from the loop road in Acadia National Park, the Shore Path in Bar Harbor and from other high viewpoints on Mt. Desert Island. Aerial sightseeing flights of the Mt. Desert area will pass over the lighthouse.

Directions: The Loop Road in Acadia National park offers distant views of this light from several scenic overlooks on the eastern side of the park. For a closer view and photographs, several tour/whale watching boats out of Bar Harbor pass this lighthouse.

Sunrise near Acadia National Park

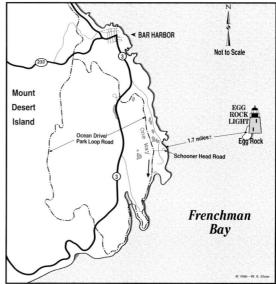

Great Duck Island Light

The Lighthouse Board recommended a light on Great Duck Island as early as 1885 but not until 1890 was the lighthouse established at the direction of President Benjamin Harrison. The wreck of a lumber schooner out of Lubec, Maine in that year may have accelerated the process. The island is located about six miles southeast of Bass Harbor and the lighthouse was intended to guide vessels into Bass Harbor or Southwest Harbor, both offering safe refuge in storms. The 42-foot granite lighthouse originally held a fifth-order Fresnel lens. Three keeper's dwellings were built side by side, along with a fog signal building; an oil house was added in 1901.

Although remote, the island once had a one-teacher school for all grades. One keeper who served from 1902-1912 had 16 children who attended along with the children of two other keepers. As many as 500 sheep also were kept on the 250-acre island, which gets its name from the abundance of waterfowl. A pond at the center of the island attracted large flocks of ducks each spring.

Legends associated with the island include a pair of seamen found frozen together, victims of a winter shipwreck. The men were buried on the island and keepers from that time honored the unknown sailors by placing a wreath on the grave each Memorial Day.

Another tale concerns a dog that survived a shipwreck, swam to Great Duck Island and was adopted by a keeper's daughter. A fisherman, the dog's original owner, returned two years later to claim his pet. As the man prepared to leave, the girl called her dog and the animal ran back as the fisherman rowed away, never to return.

The light was automated in the 1986 and the Fresnel lens replaced by a modern optic. Subsequently most all outbuildings and two keeper's homes were destroyed by the Coast Guard. In 1984 the Maine Chapter of the Nature Conservancy purchased the privately owned island. However, the Coast Guard retained jurisdiction over the light station until 1992, at which time the Conservancy gained full control of the station. The keeper's house is used as a base for ecological research and study of seabirds.

Major repairs to the tower were undertaken in 1994 and completed in the summer of 1995. Plans called for the tower to remain unpainted but mariners complained that the tower too easily blended into the adjacent outbuildings and was not clearly visible; it was repainted white in the fall of 1995. The College of the Atlantic was awarded the lightstation under auspices of the Maine Lights program. Plans call for restoration of the keeper's house for use as a research base.

Directions: The light may be seen only from the air or by boat. Whale watching trips from Bar Harbor may head in the direction of this lighthouse but the course often changes according to location of the whales.(**Note map following page**)

45

Mt. Desert Rock Light

Clearly one of the most isolated along the Maine coast, the first lighthouse on Mt. Desert Rock was built in 1830 to mark the entrances to Frenchman and Blue Hill Bays. The tiny waveswept island, approximately 600 yards long, 200 yards wide and only 17 feet above sea level at its highest point, is located some 25 nautical miles south of Mt. Desert Island.

The first structure was a short wooden tower atop a stone keeper's dwelling, with a system of eight lamps fueled by whale oil. In 1847 a new 58-foot granite tower replaced the initial weather-beaten tower; the original keeper's house remained in use until 1876. The present keeper's dwelling is the third, built in 1893. A third-order Fresnel lens was added in 1858, along with a fog bell and bell tower. Because the bell was scarcely audible above the roaring surf, it was replaced by a fog whistle in 1889. Electricity in the form of a generator came to the light and keeper's house in 1931.

Even in relatively mild storms waves wash over the island. An 1842 report by Maine's Superintendent of Lighthouses noted that a storm relocated a 57-ton granite boulder on the island; the report also mentioned that another storm moved a 75-ton boulder some 60 feet. Because the island has no topsoil, gardening was a challenge. Each spring keepers would bring barrels and bags of soil to establish vegetable and flower gardens for the summer. But with the first winter gales the results of those efforts would be washed away by the sea and the rock swept clean of all dirt and plantings.

The lantern was removed from the light in the mid 1970s to accommodate rotating aerobeacons. Public complaints and storm damage convinced the Coast Guard to install a new lantern in 1985. The last keepers were removed by helicopter in 1977 and the property was then leased to the College of the Atlantic for use as a whale watching station.

The college's Allied Whale program compiles and catalogs the North Atlantic population of finback and humpback whales. More than 4,000 individual humpback whales and 500 finbacks have been indentified. The lightstation is used as a research base when whales are feeding in that area.

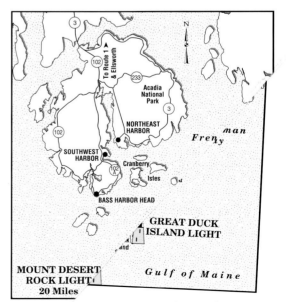

Directions: The light can be seen only by boat or by air. Whale-watching trips usually head to feeding grounds in the Mt. Desert Rock area, so the lighthouse may be seen from one of these excursions. However, because the route is determined by location of the whales, close views of the light cannot always be guaranteed. The trip to the light is approximately 1.5-2 hours each way and weather can often preclude good viewing and photography.

Bear Island Light

Bear Island is one of a group of five islands that make up the Cranberry Isles, named after the wild cranberries that once grew in abundance. A lighthouse on the southeast point of the island was authorized in 1839 by President Martin VanBuren as an aid to mariners entering Northeast Harbor. The first structure was a stone keeper's house with small

lighthouse tower on top. In 1853 a brick tower was built at one end of the dwelling; a fifth-order Fresnel lens was installed in 1858.

The present 31-foot brick lighthouse was constructed in 1889, along with a 1-1/2 story keeper's house and barn. An oil house and boathouse were later additions. The light was discontinued in 1982 and the lens removed. The property became part of Acadia National Park in 1987 but through most of the 80s the property fell into disrepair. The Friends of Acadia refurbished the keeper's house in 1989 and the tower was relighted as a private aid to navigation.

Subsequently a long-term lease was granted to a private owner in 1991 with strict stipulations regarding upkeep, restoration and repair of the property and buildings. The mailboat and ferries to the Cranberries pass this light as does the cruise from Northeast Harbor to Baker Island. The light can also be seen distantly from points along the shore.

Directions: The ferries/mailboat to Cranberry Isles pass this lighthouse.

To Northeast Harbor: From ME 3 or 233 (Eagle Lake Road), take ME 198 south to Northeast Harbor. Turn left off ME 198 in Northeast Harbor at Harbor Drive (sign indicates "marina"). Ferry/mailboat: *Sea Queen, Double B*

To Southwest Harbor: Take ME 3 or ME 233 to ME 198/102--signs clearly indicate directions. Continue on RT. 102 south to Southwest Harbor--turn left in town at the sign to upper town dock. Ferry: *Island Queen.*

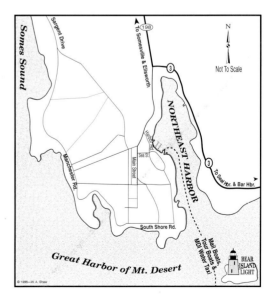

Bass Harbor Head Light

Located at the southwestern point of Mt. Desert Island, this lighthouse was built in 1858 to warn mariners of the Bass Harbor Bar at the eastern entrance to the harbor and to mark the entrance to Blue Hill Bay. Bass Harbor also offered shelter for vessels seeking refuge from easterly gales. The lighthouse is now among the most accessible and most photographed in Maine.

The brick lighthouse is attached to the 1-1/2 story wood frame keeper's house by a covered walkway. A bell tower was added in 1876 but has since been removed; a 1902 oil house remains. The original fifth-order Fresnel lens was replaced in 1902 by a fourth-order Fresnel lens which remains in the tower.

The keeper's house is the residence for the Coast Guard Commander, Southwest Harbor and is not open. Paths lead down to boulders neighboring the light station and a walkway takes you to the front of the house and the lighthouse. The view of the lighthouse from the water is much more impressive.

Directions: Follow RT 3 from Ellsworth to ME 198; turn south onto ME 102 and continue through Bass Harbor to the Coast Guard Bass Harbor Head Station entrance. There are trails east of the parking area which lead down to large granite boulders at the shore; best views and photographs of the light from land are taken from these rocks.

To get a distant view from the water: Follow "Swans Island Ferry" signs through Bass Harbor,

turning right onto Swans Island Road and the ferry landing. The ferry operates year round. This light is easily incorporated into most custom boat or air charter lighthouse routes.

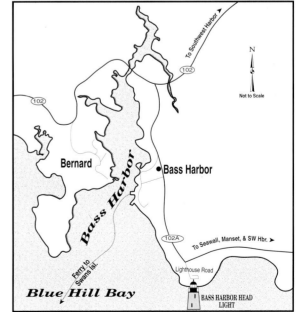

Burnt Coat Harbor Light (Hockamock Head)

Swans Island was first charted by explorer Samuel de Champlain in 1604; he named the island Brule-Cote, or "Burnt Hill." The 7,000-acre island developed strong granite, fishing and lobstering industries in the 19th century and Burnt Coat Harbor was a valued sheltered spot against wind and storms.

To mark the entrance to the harbor a lighthouse, a set of range lights originally was built on the southwest tip of Swans Island in 1872. The lights were built a distance apart, with the rear light at higher elevation; a safe channel was indicated when the lights lined up. However, after complaints that the two lights caused confusion on approaching the harbor (coupled with an increase in number of shipwrecks), the Lighthouse Board removed the smaller front range light in 1885.

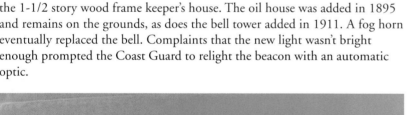

The present brick lighthouse was originally connected by a covered walkway to the 1-1/2 story wood frame keeper's house. The oil house was added in 1895 and remains on the grounds, as does the bell tower added in 1911. A fog horn eventually replaced the bell. Complaints that the new light wasn't bright enough prompted the Coast Guard to relight the beacon with an automatic optic.

The light was automated in 1975 and the original fourth-order Fresnel lens removed and replaced by an automatic light on a skeleton tower nearby.

The light station grounds are now owned by the town of Swans Island. Plans to clear trails in the area and create a park have thus far not gone forward; the keeper's house and outbuildings are in disrepair.

The island is accessible by year-round ferry from Bass Harbor with the lighthouse about four miles from the ferry landing.

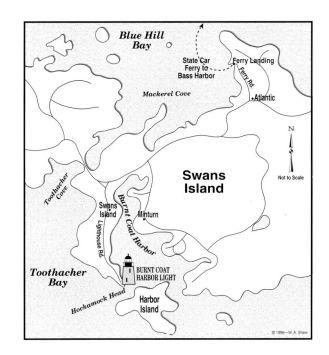

Directions: Follow "Swans Island Ferry" signs, taking ME 102 into Bass Harbor, then turn right to the ferry landing. On the island, turn right at the ferry landing, then right again at the next intersection. Continue southeast on this main road about one mile, then bear left at the fork past the Minturn turnoff into the village of Swans Island. As the road narrows, bear left and continue to a parking area at the lighthouse. A car is unnecessary as the route is an easy bicycle trip.

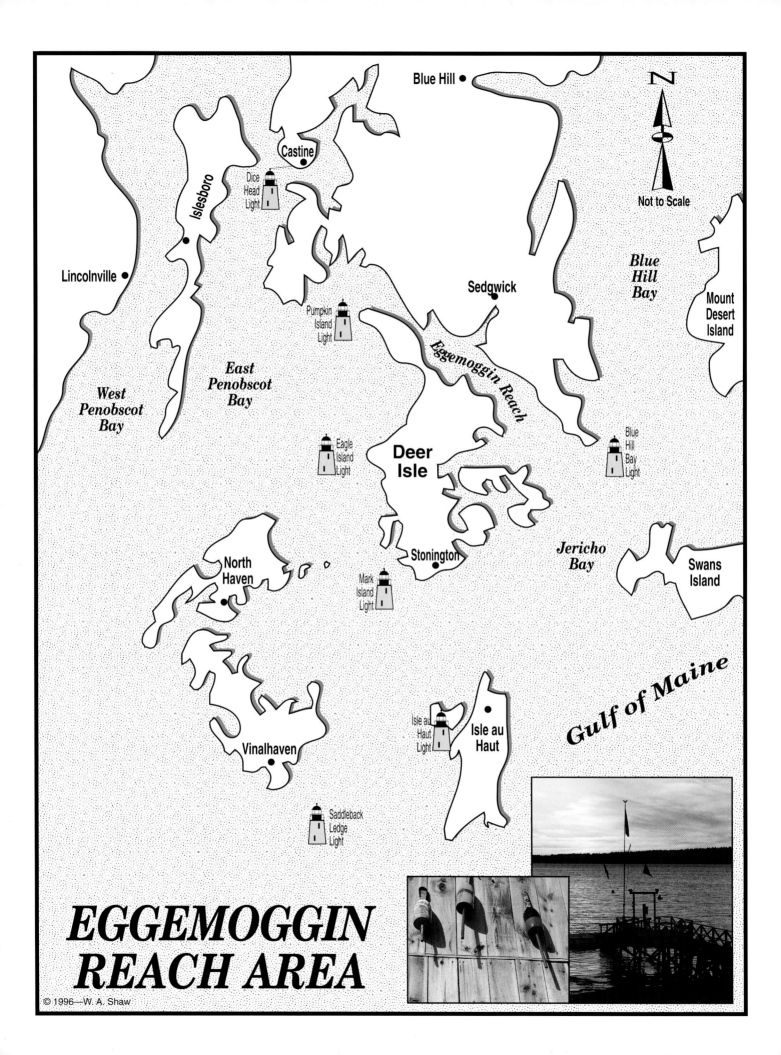

Blue Hill •

N

Not to Scale

Castine •

Islesboro

Dice
Head
Light

Lincolnville •

Blue
Hill
Bay

Sedgwick •

Mount
Desert
Island

Pumpkin
Island
Light

Eggemoggin Reach

East
Penobscot
Bay

West
Penobscot
Bay

Eagle
Island
Light

Deer
Isle

Blue
Hill
Bay
Light

North
Haven

Stonington •

Jericho
Bay

Swans
Island

Mark
Island
Light

Vinalhaven

Gulf of Maine

Isle au
Haut
Light

Isle au
Haut

Saddleback
Ledge
Light

EGGEMOGGIN REACH AREA

Saddleback Ledge Light

One of the most remote and barren of all Maine lighthouse locations, this light sits atop a rock ledge between Vinalhaven and Isle au Haut, about equidistant from each, at the southern end of Isle au Haut bay. The station was established in 1839 and the sturdy 42-foot granite tower still stands. Keeper's quarters were located inside the tower; an equipment and boathouse were added later and a fourth-order Fresnel lens added in 1856.

As on Mt. Desert Rock, the ledge had no soil so keepers at Saddleback Ledge brought soil from the mainland each spring to sustain a small vegetable and flower garden. Inevitably, however, the garden was swept away by the first winter storms.

C. 1910

Difficulty landing at this station prompted installation in 1885 of a derrick with swinging arm that held a bosun's chair on a hoist. Although a cumbersome and ungainly contraption, keepers and visitors used this means of access for many years. The conveyance could take two people at a time and reportedly became somewhat of a tourist attraction.

The light was automated in 1954, the Fresnel lens replaced by a modern optic and the attached building demolished by the Coast Guard. Views are possible only by boat or air. Photo cruises from Camden pass this light in one of the scheduled routes.

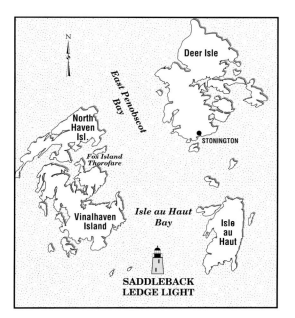

55

Deer Island Thorofare(Mark Island)Light

A strong fishing industry and booming, prosperous granite quarries in the area made the Deer Island Thorofare a busy waterway in the 19th century. The lighthouse on the west side of Mark Island guards the western approach to the Thorofare and was built in 1857 to help mariners negotiate the waters near Stonington. A 25-foot square brick tower was constructed and the tower fitted with a fourth-order Fresnel lens; keeper's house, bell tower, oil house and boathouse also were added.

The light was automated in 1958 and the Fresnel lens replaced by a modern optic. All buildings except the tower were destroyed. Although visible distantly from the mainland, the light should be viewed by boat.

C. 1910

Mark Island Light,
near Stonington, Me.

Pumpkin Island Light

Pumpkin Island, in east Penobscot Bay, marks the northern entrance to Eggemoggin Reach. In the 19th century this area was heavily travelled by vessels carrying lumber. President Franklin Pierce authorized construction of a lighthouse on the island in 1852.

First lighted in 1854, the lighthouse is a 25-foot brick tower; the lantern held a fifth-order Fresnel lens, among the earliest in Maine to be installed. A 1-1/2 story keeper's house was attached to the tower by a work shed, with an oil house added in 1904. The boathouse, dating to 1885, was enlarged in 1906. In 1889 Pumpkin Island Light was fitted with a new lantern, thereby increasing its height by three feet; a new lens was added in 1909.

The light was automated in 1930 and was among several discontinued lighthouses offered by the government at auction. The property has since had several private owners. Views are possible at the end of Eggemoggin Road on Little Deer Isle. Schooners from the Camden and Rockland area sometimes pass this light.

Directions: From U.S. Route 1 at Orland, turn south toward Castine (sign indicates Castine/Deer Isle) onto ME 175. Follow ME 175/15 south through Penobscot and Sargentville. Turn right to Little Deer Isle, continue across the Deer Island suspension bridge. Bear right at the end of the bridge (RT 15 turns left) onto Eggemoggin Road. Continue 2.6 miles to the road's end at a fishing pier near the Eggemoggin Inn. Pumpkin Island can be seen just off shore.

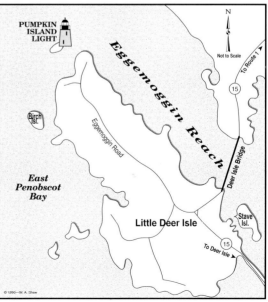

Dyce Head Light

Castine is a village whose quiet, historic elegance belies an eventful, vivid past. The town, located at the entrance to the Penobscot River, was initially settled as a trading post by the Pilgrims of Plymouth and later named after the Baron de St.Castine who took over the town in 1676. Because of its strategic location, Castine was variously occupied by the British, French and Dutch. In 1779, during the American Revolution, an entire American fleet was lost in the course of attempting to recapture Castine from the British. In the mid 19th century clipper ships regularly left Castine to trade goods around the world.

Built in 1828, Dyce Head Light was intended to guide mariners into Castine harbor and into the mouth of the Penobscot River toward Bangor. The stone tower was at one time surrounded by a six-sided wooden frame, removed by the late 19th century; in 1858 a fourth-order Fresnel lens was installed.

Dyce Head Light was discontinued in 1935 and replaced by a white skeleton tower on the north side of the harbor. The keeper's house and surrounding land became property of the town in 1937 and in 1956 the lighthouse became town property.

In April 1999 the keeper's house was partially destroyed by fire. Resoration work was completed in the summer of 2000. The keeper's house will again be rented with the income used for maintenance of the grounds. The lighthouse is easily accessible from the village; a trail leads to the front of the lighthouse and to the water.

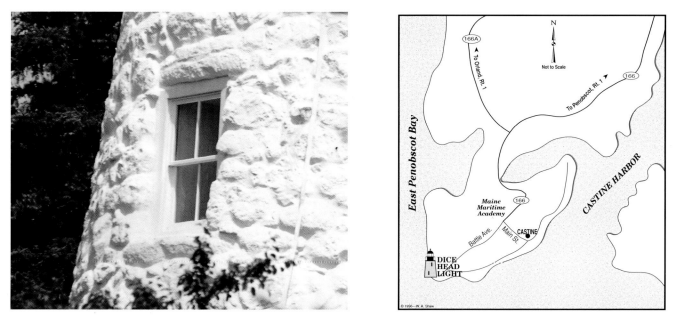

Directions: From U.S. Route 1 at Orland, take routes 175 and 166 to Castine. Continue one mile past Fort George and Maine Maritime Academy on Battle Avenue to the road's end. There is a public (marked) path to the left by the garage.

Isle au Haut Light

This island was named " Isle Haute" or "High Island" by Samuel de Champlain; a portion of the island is now a part of Acadia National Park. The lighthouse, built in 1907 at Robinson Point, was established to guide heavy shipping traffic through the Isle au Haut Thorofare, between the island and neighboring Kimball Island.

Similar to the towers built earlier at Ram Island and Marshall Point, the brick structure stands 40 feet tall on a granite base. The tower is reached via wooden walkway. A 2-1/2 story wood keeper's house and oil house also were built in 1907; the original optic was a fifth-order Fresnel lens.

The light was automated in 1934, later converted to solar power, and the property sold to private ownership. In 1986 new owners converted the keeper's house into a bed and breakfast, appropriately named "The Keeper's House Inn". The island is reached via mailboat/ferry from Stonington; the lighthouse is about 3/4 mile walk from the ferry landing. Excursion cruises from Stonington also pass the lighthouse.

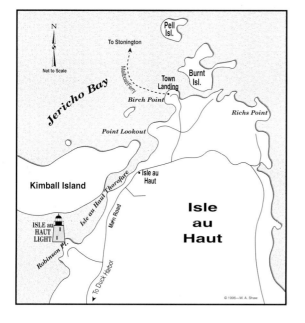

Directions: To Stonington: Take U.S. Route 1 to Orland, turning right at the sign to Castine/Deer Isle. Follow RT 175 through Penobscot, then RT 175/15 to Deer Isle into Stonington. From the Blue Hill area, follow signs to Rt. 175 and Rt. 15 to Deer Isle, then on to Stonington. Route 15 becomes Main Street; at Seabreeze Avenue turn south to the ferry dock. Parking is available at the dock area.

From the island town landing: Turn right onto the main road and walk about 3/4 mile; bear right onto a narrow path (marked with a "Keeper's House" sign). The lighthouse is about 0.5 mile ahead. Maps of the island are available in Stonington or on the mailboat. During the season, the ferry makes additonal stops at Duck Harbor on Isle au Haut.

Blue Hill Bay Light

Green Island is near the town of Brooklin, Maine west of Mt. Desert Island; it is one of four islands called the Fly or Flye Islands. On the west side of Green Island, this lighthouse was established in 1857 by order of President Franklin Pierce to guide mariners into Eggemoggin Reach connecting Penobscot Bay and the western edge of Blue Hill Bay. The lighthouse often was referred to as Eggemoggin Light or Green Island Light.

The colonial cape keeper's house was connected by brick passageway to the tower. A barn, boathouse and outhouse also were built; an oil house was added in 1905 as well as a fourth-order Fresnel lens. The lighthouse was discontinued in 1933 and replaced two years later by an automatic, solar powered light on a skeleton tower.

The property and outbuildings are now privately owned and have been carefully restored. Only about 3/4 acre at high tide, the island is about three times that size at low tide. The light must be viewed from the water.

The island at high tide......and at low tide

The light may be seen very distantly from points along shore in Brooklin but the tower is on the seaward side of the island, and trees often prohibit a clear sight even with binoculars.

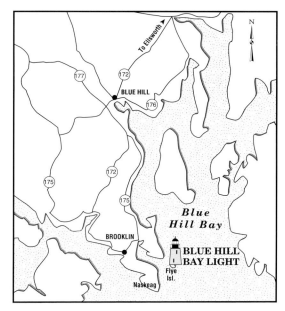

Eagle Island Light

Eagle Island is located in Penobscot Bay between Deer Isle and North Haven. Commissioned by President Van Buren in 1839, Eagle Island Light was established on the east end of the 260-acre island to guide vessels toward the Penobscot River and onto Bangor, America's leading lumber port in the mid-19th century. A wood frame, two-story keeper's house and fog bell tower were built at the same time as the stone lighthouse. An oil house was added in 1895; a fourth-order Fresnel lens was

installed in 1858. In 1932 a 4,200-pound bronze fog bell was installed in the bell tower.

The light was automated in 1959 and all buildings except the tower itself were put up for bid with the condition that the buyer remove structures from the light station property. When no one came forward, the Coast Guard in 1963 decided to raze the buildings. Members of the Quinn family, long-time residents of the island with ties to previous keepers of Eagle Island Light, appealed the decision but were unsuccessful in preventing the demolition.

In 1964 all buildings were razed, leaving the tower scarred and only traces of the old foundations remaining. When trying to remove the giant fog bell, the demolition crew lost control of it and the bell careened down the cliff into the ocean. An unexpecting lobsterman later found the bell and retrieved it; photographer Eliot Porter subsequently purchased the bell.

The lighthouse is now on private property and access to the island carefully controlled. Views from the water are partially obscured by trees. Excursion trips around, not onto, the island are offered via the mailboat from Sunset, Maine or from cruises out of Camden, Maine.

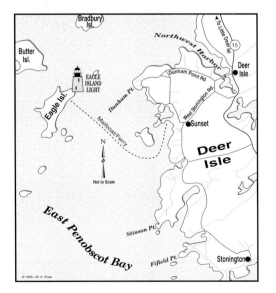

Directions: Via mailboat out of Sunset, Maine. Take RT 15 into Deer Isle and turn right at the post office (marked with a "Sunset" sign), bear right again at Pressey Village Road (0.5mile), then left onto Dunham Point Road. Continue on to Sylvester Cove (about 3.2 miles from the post office).

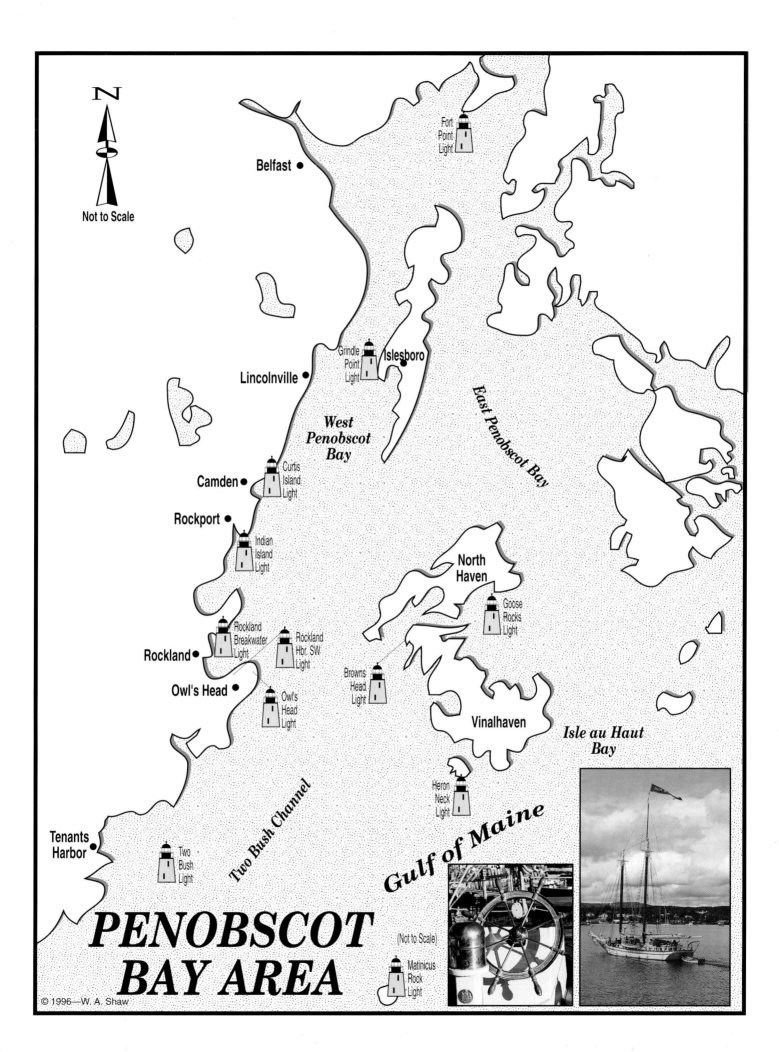

N

Not to Scale

Fort
Point
Light

Belfast •

Grindle
Point
Light

Islesboro

Lincolnville •

*West
Penobscot
Bay*

East Penobscot Bay

Curtis
Island
Light

Camden •

Rockport •

Indian
Island
Light

North
Haven

Goose
Rocks
Light

Rockland
Breakwater
Light

Rockland
Hbr. SW.
Light

Rockland •

Browns
Head
Light

Owl's Head •

Owl's
Head
Light

Vinalhaven

*Isle au Haut
Bay*

Heron
Neck
Light

Tenants
Harbor •

Two
Bush
Light

Two Bush Channel

Gulf of Maine

(Not to Scale)

Matinicus
Rock
Light

PENOBSCOT
BAY AREA

© 1996—W. A. Shaw

Fort Point Light

At the west side of the mouth of the Penobscot River in Stockton Springs, Fort Point Light was established in 1836 by order of President Andrew Jackson to aid vessels bound for Bangor, a leading lumber port. The lighthouse got its name from adjacent Fort Pownall, built in 1759 to guard against the French, by order of Massachusetts Governor Pownall (Maine was at that time a part of Massachusetts).

The first wooden tower was replaced by the present 31-foot square brick lighthouse in 1857; a two-story keepers house, attached to the tower, was built in the same year. In 1890 a bell tower was added and in 1897 and oil house built. All buildings still remain, with the pyramidal bell tower listed on the National Register of Historic Places. Replaced by a fog horn, the bell now hangs outside the tower; the 1857 Fresnel lens remains in use.

The light was automated in 1988; the grounds and buildings are now part of Fort Point State Park. The lighthouse is easily accessible with nearby parking.

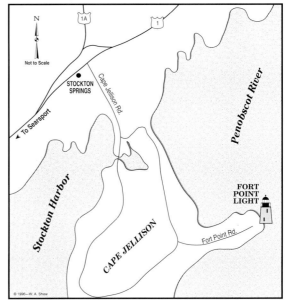

Directions: From U.S. Route 1 at Stockton Springs, take the turn marked "Stockton Springs". Continue about 0.5 mile through the small town and follow the Fort Point State Park sign, turning right onto East Cape Road. Follow that road to the park entrance; the park road is clearly marked and leads to a small parking area near the lighthouse. Also, the next road left after the park entrance leads directly to the lighthouse and a small parking area just outside the grounds.

Grindle Point Light

Islesboro is a 10-mile long narrow island in upper Penobscot Bay. The largest 19th century commercial shipping fleet in the bay was based at Islesboro. Located on the north side of the entrance to Gilkey Harbor, the original 28-foot tower was established in 1851 built on three acres of land purchased from Francis Grindle who became the second keeper in April 1853.

The tower was rebuilt in 1874 after succumbing to the elements, a 39-foot square brick tower attached by covered walkway to the 1-1/2 story keeper's house. Both structures still remain. A fifth-order Fresnel lens was installed; a boathouse was added in 1886 and an oil house in 1906. In 1934 Grindle Point Light was deactivated and replaced by a nearby skeleton light tower. The grounds and lighthouse became property of the town of Islesboro.

Fifty three years later, Islesboro residents convinced the Coast Guard to recomission Grindle Point lighthouse in 1987; a solar-powered optic was installed and the skeleton tower removed. The Islesboro Sailor's Memorial Museum is now located in the keeper's house and the 1881 fogbell on the south side of the light tower is on loan from the Shore Village Museum in Rockland, Maine. Although distantly visible from the mainland, the ferry between Lincolnville and Islesboro docks next to the lighthouse; the three-mile crossing takes 20 minutes each way.

Directions: Route 1 to Lincolnville (north from Camden, south from Belfast). Follow signs to Islesboro Ferry. There is parking adjacent to the ferry landing. The lighthouse is at the ferry landing on Islesboro.

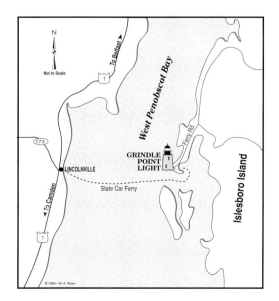

Goose Rocks Light

Goose Rocks Light was established in 1890 to mark the east entrance to the Fox Islands Thorofare, a busy waterway between Vinalhaven and North Haven islands. The structure is a typical caisson-type or "sparkplug" style, cast-iron lighthouse of that era, built on a circular foundation filled with concrete. Lubec Channel and Spring Point Ledge lights also are of this type.

The 51-foot tower has three stories inside and originally had a fourth-order Fresnel lens. In 1963 the light was automated, the lens replaced with a 250mm modern optic and subsequently converted to solar power. Although visible distantly from Vinalhaven, the light is best viewed by boat. (***Note map accompanying Browns Head Light for location***).

Curtis Island Light

In the early 1600s Captain John Smith arrived in Camden harbor. With him on the voyage was a black cook who allowed that if he could have any place in the world, the small island would be the place. Captain Smith then awarded the cook ownership, whereupon the island became "Negro Island".More than 200 years later, the first brick lighthouse on the five-acre island at the entrance to Camden Harbor was built in 1835 by order of President Andrew Jackson.

Marking the south side of the harbor entrance, the initial tower was replaced with the present 25-foot brick tower in 1896. The keeper's house had been rebuilt in 1889 and a boathouse added. A fourth-order Fresnel lens also was installed.

Original lens

(Continued)

Curtis Island Light

The island's name was changed in 1934 to Curtis Island in memory of Cyrus H.K. Curtis, publisher of the Saturday Evening Post and longtime summer resident and benefactor of Camden. In 1972 the light was automated and the Fresnel lens removed; the town of Camden acquired the property surrounding the lighthouse the following year. The island is a city park and open to visitors but is accessible only by small boat.

Although there are several locations along the shore offering distant views of this light, it is best seen and photographed by boat or air. Any of the sight-seeing or windjammer cruises departing from the Camden Harbor public landing will pass immediately in front of the lighthouse and afford excellent views.

Directions: U.S. Route 1 to Camden. Turn onto Bayview Street, then left to the town warf. Arrangements may be made to go to Curtis Island for the day or for a few hours to enjoy the park. The light also may be seen well in winter through the trees further up Bayview Street; the drives are private property and there is no access to the shorefront.

Browns Head Light

Vinalhaven is part of a group called the Fox Islands after the grey foxes that once lived there in abundance. Located 12 miles from Rockland in the middle of Penobscot Bay, the island was named for John Vinal. Maine was then a part of Massachusetts and Vinal lobbied the state legislature to incorporate the island as a town in 1789.

Today the island supports a substantial fishing and lobstering industry but in the 19th century the granite industry was the mainstay of the local economy. Increased shipping traffic associated with this industry prompted President Andrew Jackson to authorize construction of Browns Head Light in 1832 . The light is located on the northwest point of Vinalhaven, marking the western entrance to the Fox Islands Thorofare.

The keeper's house was in disrepair in 1857 and a new 1-1/2 story wood-framed house was built, connected by a covered walkway to the 20-foot tower. A fifth-order Fresnel lens was installed in that year as was a bell tower with 1,000-pound fog bell. In 1987 Browns Head Light was among the last lighthouses in Maine to be automated.

On Vinalhaven

The Fresnel lens was removed at that time; the bell tower was destroyed for no apparent reason after the automation. The bell is now displayed by the Vinalhaven Historical Society. Light station grounds were leased to the town of Vinalhaven and the town manager currently lives in the keeper's house.

Directions: Take the ferry from Rockland to Vinalhaven. Coming off the ferry, turn right and follow Main and High Streets to North Haven Road. Turn right and continue for about six miles;be careful to keep track of mileage as there are no street signs or markers to the light. Look for a group of mailboxes at the intersection with a dirt road (Crockett River Road); turn left onto that road, then right at the second dirt road to the right. There is a small sign pointing to the lighthouse. Pass a small cemetery on the right. There is a small parking area at the light.

Additionally, the Goose Rocks Lighthouse can be seen in the distance from Calderwood Point on Calderwood Neck. The road is unimproved; hiking to the point, rather than driving, is recommended. Both lights are easily viewed by boat from the Fox Islands Thorofare.

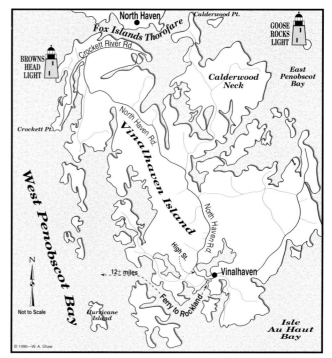

Heron Neck Light

On the southern tip of Green Island, just southwest of Carver's Harbor on Vinalhaven, this light was built in 1854 to mark the east entrance to Hurricane Sound. The 30-foot brick tower located on a sharply defined rock ledge, was attached to the brick keeper's house by a passageway; a fifth-order Fresnel lens was installed. The keeper's house was rebuilt in 1895, an oil house (still standing) added in 1903 and fog bell tower in 1944. A fog horn subsequently replaced the bell; the horn is displayed at the Shore Village Museum in Rockland.

Heron Neck Light was automated in 1982 and a new plastic 300mm lens replaced the Fresnel. In April of 1989 an electrical fire severely damaged the empty keeper's house but fortunately the lighthouse tower was spared. Shortly thereafter in 1990 the Coast Guard confirmed there was no intent to rebuild the dwelling. This decision received national publicity and in 1992 a Boston developer offered to restore the structure. Citing an engineering survery stating that restoration of the keeper's house to its original condition would be impossible, the Coast Guard then announced plans to raze the building.

Preservationists objected to that plan and battle of conflicting opinions/
intents/interpretations ensued, each group claiming to offer the best
course of action. An agreement was reached whereby the Coast Guard
turned over the light station to the Island Institute of Rockland. The
Institute in turn leased the property an individual who restored the
damaged keeper's house; the work is ongoing.

In 1989 the owner of Green Island unofficially
renamed the island "Bush Island" after then
President George Bush. Outward Bound's
Hurricane Island is "next door".

The lighthouse must be viewed by boat or air.
Windjammer cruises from Camden, Rockport or
Rockland often pass this light; specialty photo
excursion tours from Camden also pass Heron
Neck Light.

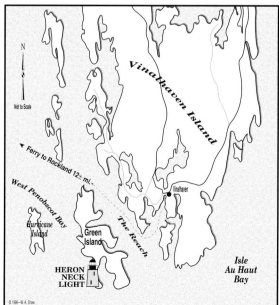

Indian Island Light

The first Indian Island Light, established in 1850 at the east entrance to Rockport Harbor, was a lantern mounted on the roof of the keeper's house. A fourth-order Fresnel lens was installed in 1856. After being discontinued for a time, the light was reactivated and a new lighthouse tower was built in 1875.

The present lighthouse is a square brick tower attached to the original 1-1/2 story T-shaped brick keeper's house. The light was discontinued permanently in 1934 and replaced by an automatic light on nearby Lowell rock. Since that time the property has been privately owned. Although visible distantly from Rockport Marine Park and other points on shore in the Beauchamp Point area, the light is best viewed from excursion boats and schooners from Camden, Rockport and Rockland.

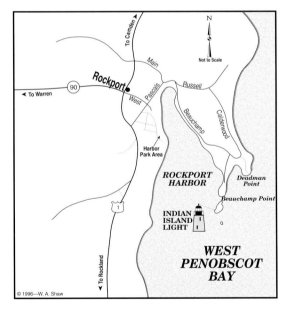

Directions: In Rockport at the intersection of U.S. 1 and ME 90, turn east onto West Street. Continue to Pascals Avenue and turn left, **crossing** the Goose River Bridge. Turn around and bear left just past the bridge into the Rockport Marine Park entrance (clearly marked). There is a parking area down the hill. **Or..** From Camden, follow Chestnut St. then Russell Ave. to Beauchamp Point. The road becomes a dirt road and, although narrow, there are areas to park. The area is lovely and the lighthouse can be seen in the distance.

Two Bush Island Light

This island takes its name from two solitary pine trees which served as day beacons before the 42-foot square lighthouse was built in 1897. Located just outside the west side of Penobscot Bay, almost directly south of Owls Head, this light marks the north end of Two Bush Channel and the east side entrance to the Muscle Ridge Channel, a principal sea lane to west Penobscot Bay. The trees are long gone and the location remains among the more lonely and isolated along the Maine coast.

Legend tells of a keeper's dog named Smut who was involved in a heroic rescue. The story tells that, during a snow storm, a fishing schooner was in danger of being smashed on the rocky shores of the island. The fishermen had taken to a dory as a leak opened on the vessel. When trying to find a way to land at Two Bush, they heard Smut barking. Alerted by the dog's commotion, the keeper ran to the shore and saw the two men in the dory. Although their boat was overturned by a wave, the fishermen were hauled ashore by the keeper and his assistant. Smut welcomed the visitors with licks and both mariners offered to buy the dog at any price. The keeper refused to sell his pet. Two Bush Light was automated in 1964; in 1970 the Coast Guard allowed the Green Berets to destroy the keeper's house as a demolition exercise. Today the light stands alone on the stark island and must be photographed by boat or air.

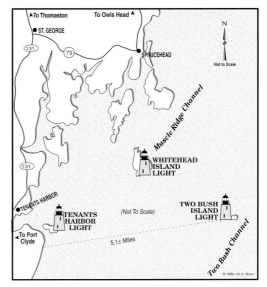

Rockland Breakwater Light

A small lantern was placed at Jameson Point at the entrance to Rockland Harbor in 1827. As Rockland became a leading port for export of lime rock in the late 19th century, it became apparent that a lighthouse was necessary. The 0.8 mile-long stone jetty was built between 1881 and 1899; as the work progressed in piecemeal fashion, dependent upon allocation of funds, the small beacon was moved further out as the breakwater extended. In 1902 a permanent lighthouse was built at the breakwater's end and a 25-foot brick tower was added atop the roof of the brick keeper's house. A fourth-order Frensel lens was installed. The light was automated in 1964 and in 1973 the Coast Guard announced plans to raze the structure. This news was not well received, prompting the nearby Samoset Resort to assume partial responsibility for upkeep of the dwelling. However, in 1989 the resort relinquished its involvement. Major renovations were completed in 1990.

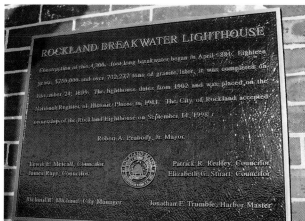

In 1998, responsibility for maintenance of the station was assigned to the American Lighthouse Foundation. Extensive restoration and renovation are ongoing; the keeper's house will be furnished and open to the public when the work is complete. Although the walk along the breakwater takes you directly to the lighthouse, best views and photographs are from the water. Ferries from Rockland pass this light as do area excursion boats and schooners.

Directions: From U.S. Route 1, turn onto Waldo Avenue ("Samoset Resort" sign). Continue for about 0.5 mile, turning right at Samoset road. The road ends at parking area. The breakwater, to the left of a small park area, leads about 0.8 mile to the lighthouse. The Maine State Ferries from Rockland to Vinalhaven and North Haven pass close to this light. Additionally, Rockland is home to many of Maine's windjammers. A trip aboard any of these vessels takes you by Rockland Breakwater light and oftentimes other lighthouses in Penobscot Bay.

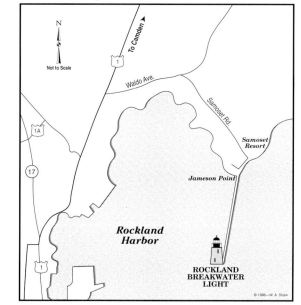

81

Matinicus Rock Light

Matinicus Rock is an isolated, barren 32-acre granite island about five miles southeast of Matinicus Island, 25 miles from Rockland, the nearest port. This location experiences some of the most violent Atlantic weather, is fogbound approximately 20% of the year and is continuously scoured by waves. The lighthouse, located on the south side of the Rock, is probably the most isolated station along the Maine coast, halfway between Monhegan Island and Mt. Desert Island and 22 miles south of the entrance to Penobscot Bay.

The prominent location on approach to the Bay prompted President John Quincy Adams to authorize construction of two lighthouses on Matinicus Rock in 1827.

Twin wooden towers initially were built 40 feet apart, each at the end of a stone dwelling. In 1846 a new granite keeper's house was constructed; two years later new granite towers were added, 60 yards apart.

A 2,000-pound fog bell was added in 1855 and replaced in 1869 by one of the first steam-driven fog whistles. Both towers were rebuilt in 1857 and a third-order Fresnel lens installed in each. The north light was discontinued in 1883, but the single light proved unsatisfactory and in 1888 the second light was reinstated.

In 1924 Matinicus Rock became a single light station (north light again discontinued) by government order, as did all twin-light stations. Following a violent storm in 1950, the station's outbuildings and old keeper's house were removed; the light was automated in 1983 and the Fresnel lens removed. The two towers, keeper's house and an 1890 oil house now remain.

Although there are many tales of heroism by the keepers of Matinicus Rock Light, the best known is that of 17-year-old Abbie Burgess. Her story is arguably foremost among lighthouse legends; she is credited with saving her three sisters and mother during a violent storm in January 1856. Her father became keeper at The Rock in 1853 and brought with him an invalid wife and five children.

The oldest girl, 14-year-old Abbie, learned to tend the lamps and by age 17 was regularly looking after the lights while her father went lobster fishing to augment his income. In January 1856, her father left for the mainland for provisions; a violent storm soon developed. Abbie took her family into the base of the lighthouse for safety as the storm swept away the keeper's house.

(Continued)

Matinicus Rock Light

While rough seas kept her father away for a month, Abbie tended the lights and cared for her family. She later married Issac Grant, the son of the light keeper

who replaced her father, and was appointed assistant keeper at Matinicus Rock. Abbie, her husband and four children were transferred to the Whitehead Light station in 1875 where they served for 15 years. In 1892 Abbie Grant died at the age of 53; at the foot of her grave in Forest Hill Cemetery (off ME 73 between South Thomaston and St. George) is a small stone replica of a lighthouse.

"The Rock" is home to a nesting colony of Atlantic Puffins, as well as terns and other sea birds. The lighthouse must be viewed by boat or air. Trips departing from Rockland offer a chance to see whales and, in season, puffins in surrounding waters.

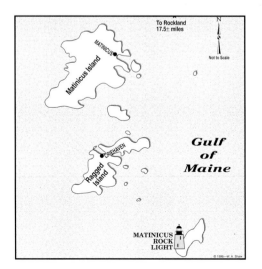

84

Owls Head Light

The growing lime trade in nearby Rockland and Thomaston warranted construction of a lighthouse on Owls Head at the entrance to Rockland Harbor. President John Quincy Adams authorized the work in 1825. The 20-foot brick tower is unusually short; the height of the promontory made a tall lighthouse unnecessary, still putting the light at 100 feet above sea level. A fourth-order Fresnel lens was installed in 1856.

Legend tells that, during a storm in December 1850, a small schooner from Massachusetts broke lose from its mooring at Jameson Point and headed across Penobscot Bay toward Owls Head. The captain had gone ashore leaving the mate, a

seaman and one passenger aboard. As the storm intensified, the vessel smashed into the rocky ledges south of the lighthouse; the three on board huddled together, wrapped in blankets against the freezing surf.

As the schooner broke apart, the seaman left the vessel, managed get ashore and reached the road to the lighthouse. The keeper happened to be driving by in a sleigh, took the dazed man to his house and learned of the others still at sea. A rescue party located the schooner and found a block of ice enveloping the mate and passenger. After bringing the block ashore, carefully chipping away the ice and slowly warming the victims, both revived. The mate, Richard Ingraham and passenger, Lydia Dyer, were later married. The seaman died soon after the wreck.

Another well-known tale associated with Owls Head light is that of springer spaniel, Spot. The dog learned to pull the fog bell rope with his teeth when he saw an approaching vessel. Boats would answer with a whistle or bell and Spot would bark reply. One stormy night in the 1890s, the mailboat from Matinicus was headed toward Owls Head. The fog bell rope was buried in the snow but Spot's constant barking warned the captain in time to guide his vessel around the peninsula, clear the rocks, and sound a whistle to acknowledge safe passage. The spaniel is buried on the hillside near the former location of the fog bell.

(Continued)

The 1854 keeper's house remains a residence for Coast Guard personnel and the surrounding grounds are now a state park. The bell tower is gone but the 1895 oil house remains. The lighthouse is easily accessible with parking nearby; ferries and excursion boats also pass the light.

Owls Head Light

Directions: From U.S. Route 1 in Thomaston/ Rockland, turn south onto ME 73 and continue about two miles, turning left onto North Shore Drive. Go about 2.5 miles, turning left just past the Owl's Head post office, onto Main Street. Continue to Lighthouse Road (marked) and turn left; the road becomes a dirt road and leads to a parking and picnic area. A short walk takes you to the lighthouse. The keeper's house is occupied by a Coast Guard family.

Ferries, harbor tour boats, windjammers and charter boat excursions all pass this light.

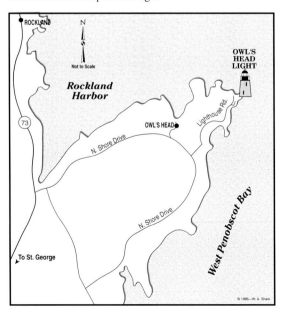

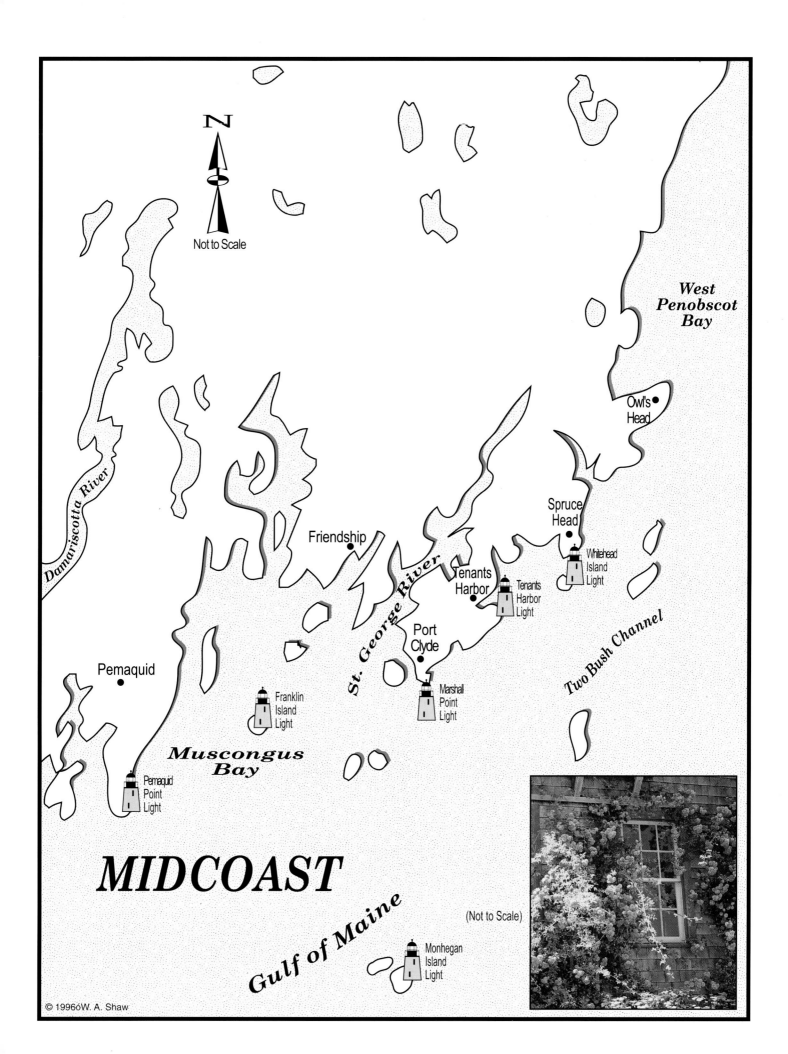

N

Not to Scale

West
Penobscot
Bay

Owl's
Head

Damariscotta River

Spruce
Head

Friendship

Whitehead
Island
Light

St. George River

Tenants
Harbor

Tenants
Harbor
Light

Pemaquid

Port
Clyde

Two Bush Channel

Franklin
Island
Light

Marshall
Point
Light

Muscongus
Bay

Pemaquid
Point
Light

MIDCOAST

Gulf of Maine

(Not to Scale)

Monhegan
Island
Light

© 1996ó W. A. Shaw

Whitehead Light

President Thomas Jefferson ordered construction of this lighthouse in 1807. Located on a small island near Tenants Harbor, this light marks the western entrance to the Muscle Ridge Channel. The original lighthouse and keeper's dwelling were stone structures. Because this area is covered in fog approximately 20% of the year, a fog signal was installed in 1839. The signal was continuously operated by a striking mechanism of timbers, chains and weights which was wound, then driven by the rise and fall of the tide. The "perpetual fog bell" was well received by mariners but, by 1842, storm damage to the complex mechanism meant the keeper was again responsible for sounding the fog bell. A steam-driven whistle was installed in the 1860s.

In 1852, a new, 41-foot lighthouse and new wooden keeper's house replaced the initial structures; a third-order Fresnel lens was installed in 1857. Whitehead was the first Maine light station to have a one-room school house and teacher, with more than 30 children, some from nearby islands, in attendance. The teacher boarded with the keeper's family.

Tales associated with this light include that of two shipwrecked sailors who froze to death on Whitehead in 1805; their graves remain on the island. Another involves the first lighthouse keeper, Ellis Dolph, who initiated a side business by selling the whale oil intended for the light. As the orders for oil steadily increased, officials became suspicious; investigation revealed that storekeepers in nearby Thomaston had been buying entire barrels of oil from the keeper. Dolph's duties were summarily terminated.

Whitehead Island is perhaps most well known for one of its assistant keepers. In 1875 Issac Grant became keeper of the light; his assistant, and wife, was Abbie Burgess Grant, heroine of Matinicus Rock. Their son took over as keeper in 1890; the station would later become a "stag" light instead of a family station.

The light was automated in 1982 and the Fresnel lens replaced with a modern optic.

Difficult to see even distantly from shore, the lighthouse must be viewed by boat or air. Photo cruises from Camden pass this light. The island has walking paths if you're able to land with skiff or kayak.

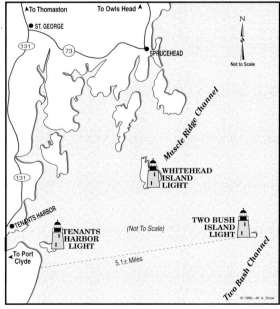

Tenants Harbor Light

Known among area residents as "Jamie Wyeth's place", the lighthouse is located at the east end of 22-acre Southern Island at the harbor entrance. The 27-foot brick tower was built in 1857 and is connected to the keeper's house by a passageway. A fourth-order Fresnel lens was originally installed and an oil house added in 1906.

The pyramidal bell tower now serves as Wyeth's studio. The light was discontinued in 1934 and offered at auction; several owners preceded the purchase by Andrew Wyeth. His son, Jamie, now owns the property. The lighthouse and keeper's dwelling have been restored and beautifully maintained.

Although the buildings can be seen distantly from the public landing at Tenants Harbor, trees often obscure any view of the lighthouse; best viewing is by boat as the lighthouse is on the eastern side of the island. Specialty excursions from Camden to view lights in the Muscle Ridge Channel pass this lighthouse.

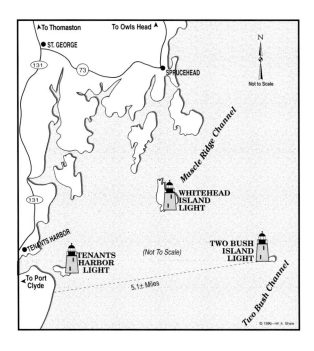

90

Marshall Point Light

Marking the eastern side of the south entrance to Port Clyde Harbor, this lighthouse was built in 1832. At that time the village of Port Clyde was a major port, with granite quarries, shipbuilding facilities and fish canning operations. The initial structure was a 20-foot tall rubblestone tower. In 1857 the present 31-foot brick and granite lighthouse was built with a fifth-order Fresnel lens installed. The lighthouse is connected to the shore by a wooden walkway and resembles the Isle au Haut and Ram Island Lights. A bell tower with 1,000-pound bronze bell was added in 1898 and remained in use until it was replaced by a horn in 1969. The original 1832 keeper's house was destroyed by lightning in 1895 and replaced with the present dwelling.

In 1971 the light was automated, the Fresnel lens removed and a Loran navigation station set up in the keeper's house. When that equipment became outdated in 1980, the dwelling was boarded up. Subsequently, the property was acquired by the Town of St. George. Restoration of the structure was undertaken in 1986 by the Marshall Point Restoration Committee. Grants of more than $100,000 from the National Park Service Bicentennial Lighthouse Fund, matched by the Town of St. George and public contributions, were used by the St. George Historical Society to accomplish the restoration.

The keeper's house was placed on the National Register of Historic Places in 1988 and the initial restoration completed in 1990.

(Continued)

The Marshall Point Lighthouse Museum displays memorabilia relating to the town and three area lighthouses: Tenants Harbor, Whitehead and Marshall Point. Most recently the summer kitchen has been rebuilt as an addition to the museum; future plans include rebuilding of the bell tower and outbuildings.

Inside the keeper's house/museum; the case displays miniature lobster buoys identifying local fishermen.

Marshall Point Light

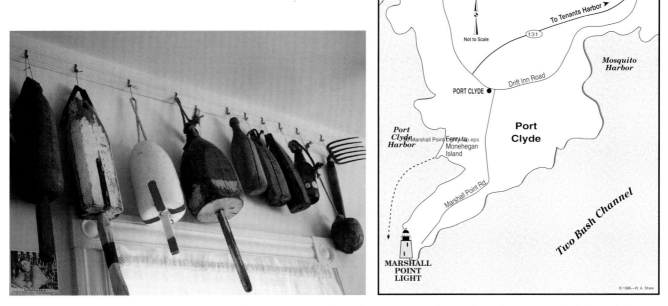

Directions: From U.S.Route 1 in Thomaston, take ME 131 south through St. George and Tenant's Harbor to Port Clyde. Turn left at the "Marshall Point Museum" sign (Dick Cliff Road). Continue up the hill, passing another sign for the museum, and turn right onto Marshall Point Road. Pass a "Dead End" sign and two stone pillars on either side of the narrowing road. The road ends at the lighthouse parking area. The passenger ferry Elizabeth Ann out of Port Clyde to Monhegan Island passes this light.

Franklin Island Light

Five miles offshore from the village of Friendship, Maine, this light was built in 1803 by order of President Thomas Jefferson, making it Maine's third oldest lighthouse. Lack of supplies and foul weather combined to delay completion of the construction until 1807. The light replaced a day marker placed as a navigational aid and was intended to warn vessels away from nearby rocks in Muscongus Bay. A fourth-order Fresnel lens was installed.

Located on the northwest side of the island, only the 45-foot brick tower remains; the structure initially was attached to the keeper's house. That dwelling and other outbuildings except the oil house were dismantled by the Coast Guard when the light was automated in 1967.

This light can be photographed only by boat or air.

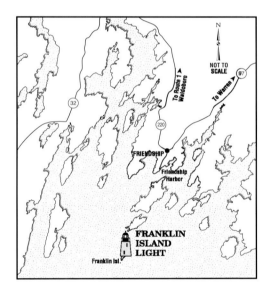

Pemaquid Point Light

Offering at once some of the most majestic, stark, and striking scenery on the Maine coast, this lighthouse sits atop unique rock formations which reflect the result of waves pounding this area in strong storms. Commissioned in 1827 by John Quincy Adams, this light is located at the west side of the entrance to Muscongus Bay.

The original lighthouse was of faulty construction and therefore replaced by a 38-foot stone tower in 1835; a fourth-order Fresnel lens was added in 1856. A wooden keeper's house replaced the initial stone structure in 1857. The fog bell house and tower were constructed in 1897 and included a hand-cranked mechanism which powered the striking machinery. In 1934 the bell was removed; storms destroyed the house and tower in 1991 but both were reconstructed the following year.

(Continued)

95

Pemaquid Point Light

During the years 1903-1917 four major shipwrecks occurred on the rocks at Pemaquid Point, most notable among them the British vessel *Angel Gabriel*. The light, visible on a clear day for 14 miles, was the first in Maine to be automated in 1934.

The keeper's house now houses the Fishermen's Museum which is operated by the Town of Bristol, displaying artifacts of Maine lighthouses and the fishing/lobster industry. A park area is adjacent to the lighthouse grounds, easily accessible with parking.

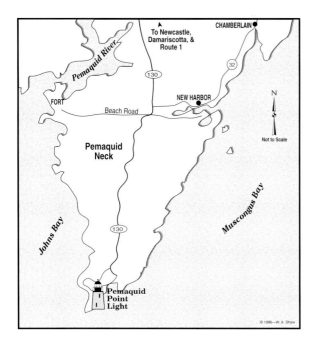

Directions: From U.S. Route 1 in Damariscotta, turn onto ME 129/130, then follow ME 130 south to its end at Pemaquid Point. Alternatively, from U.S. 1 in Waldoboro, turn south onto ME 32 and follow that route through New Harbor to the junction with ME 130. Turn south (left) onto ME 130 and follow the road to its end at Pemaquid Point. To view the lighthouse by boat, cruises are available out of Boothbay Harbor or from Maine Maritime Museum in Bath.

"Near this site on August 14, 1635
John Cogswell and family from
Westbury Leigh, Wietshire, England
first set foot in America.
They arrived on the ship *Angel Gabriel*
which was wrecked here on the
following day in a violent storm. The
family settled in Ipswich, Massachusetts."

Monhegan Island Light

Ten miles off the coast, Monhegan Island was originally settled in 1614, offering a safe haven from Indians; the first permanent European settlement was established in 1619. However, some historians suggest that rock carvings on nearby Manana Island indicate the Vikings visited the area around 1,000 A.D. Monhegan is 1.5 miles long, 0.5 mile wide and represents Maine's first fishing village, with its permanent residents still primarily engaged in the fishing and lobstering industry. To avoid over fishing, Monhegan lobster season is limited to the winter months, January to June, with New Year's Day (or thereabouts depending on the weather) being "Trap Day", one of the year's major occasions. For their work in the most challenging weather conditions, Monhegan fishermen benefit from significantly higher lobster prices during this time.

Since Monhegan Island was the first point sighted on most trans-Atlantic voyages and a well-known landmark for seafarers, it was logical a lighthouse should be located here. The first granite lighthouse, located near the center of the island at the island's highest elevation, was built in 1824. A wooden keeper's house also was constructed. The present 48-foot granite tower replaced the original structure in 1850. This lighthouse is the second highest above water on the Maine coast at 178 feet; only Seguin is higher at 180 feet.

A new two-story keeper's house was added in 1874; a second-order Fresnel lens was installed in 1856. The fog bell installed at Monhegan was unsatisfactory since the signal volume couldn't be increased enough to be heard offshore. Following several failed attempts to adjust the volume, a trumpet was installed at Manana Island. The keeper at Monhegan pushed a button which alerted the Fog Signal keeper on Manana.

In 1959 the light was automated and is now controlled from the Coast Guard station on Manana Island, across the harbor. The fog signal also is now automated. In 1962 the lighthouse grounds and buildings, except the lighthouse tower, were sold to the Monhegan Associates. A museum was opened in the keeper's house in 1968, with the station's original fog bell on display.

Assistant Keeper's House

The Monhegan Historical and Cultural Museum Association took over responsibility for the property in 1985. The group recently supervised reconstruction of the assistant keeper's house to serve as an art museum.

(Continued)

Monhegan Island Light

Reportedly more than six hundred varieties of wild flowers can be found on Monhegan, with more than two hundred bird species logged. The island also has become a summer art colony, and has, in past years, attracted writers, naturalists and artists including Andrew and Jamie Wyeth, Rockwell Kent, George Bellows and Andrew Winter.

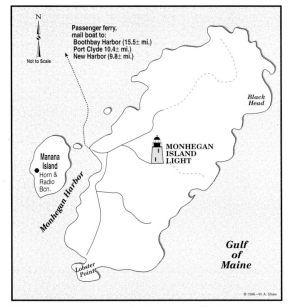

Directions: Monhegan Island is reached by boat from either Boothbay Harbor, New Harbor or Port Clyde.

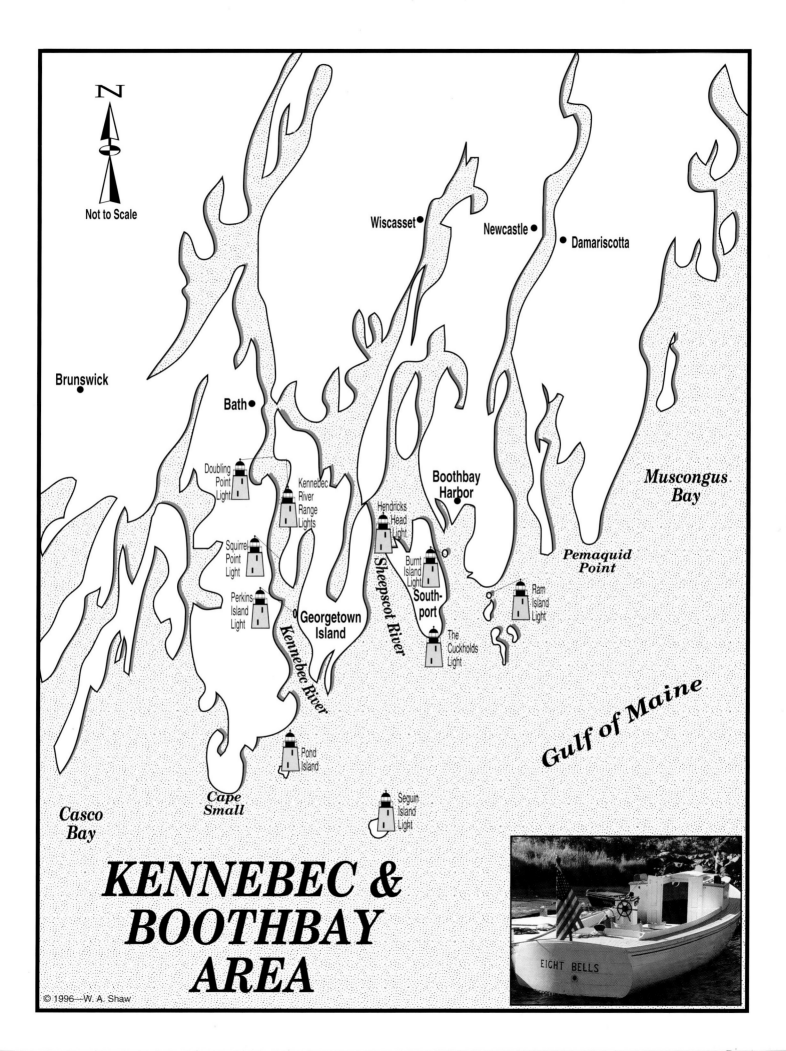

N

Not to Scale

Wiscasset ●

Newcastle ●

● Damariscotta

Brunswick
●

Bath ●

*Muscongus
Bay*

Doubling
Point Light

Kennebec
River
Range
Lights

**Boothbay
Harbor**

Squirrel
Point
Light

Hendricks
Head
Light

*Pemaquid
Point*

Perkins
Island
Light

Burnt
Island
Light

Southport

Ram
Island
Light

○ **Georgetown
Island**

Sheepscot River

Kennebec River

The
Cuckholds
Light

Gulf of Maine

Pond
Island

*Cape
Small*

Seguin
Island
Light

*Casco
Bay*

KENNEBEC &
BOOTHBAY
AREA

© 1996—W. A. Shaw

EIGHT BELLS

Burnt Island Light

Construction of Burnt Island light, the tenth lighthouse established in Maine, was authorized byPresident James Monroe. Located on the west side of the entrance to Boothbay Harbor, this lighthouse was built in 1821. The 30-foot stone lighthouse was accompanied by a wood keeper's house which was razed in1857 and replaced by a 1-1/2 story cottage. In the 1850s the tower's lantern was enlarged to accommodate installation of a fourth-order Fresnel lens. A walkway between the tower and house also was added in 1857; the boathouse and oil house that remain were built in 1880 and 1899 respectively. A bell tower with 1,000-pound fog bell was added in 1895.

Confusion with the light from the Cuckolds Light in the outer harbor prompted addition of a dark sector to the light in 1888; this code was changed in 1892 to the present red flashing light with white sectors. After this change ships were not attracted over the rocks at the Cuckholds which were in the path to Burnt Island Light. Burnt Island Light became the last lighthouse in New England to be converted from kerosene to electricity in April 1962. In 1989 the light was among the last in Maine to be automated; the Fresnel lens had been previously removed.

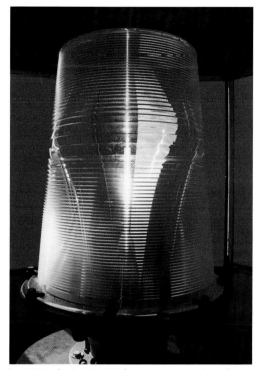

In 1998, the Maine Lights program assigned responsibility for the lighthouse to the Maine Department of Marine Resources. Since that time extensive repairs and renovation work have been ongoing; exterior and site work were completed in 2000, with interior restoration scheduled for 2001. The island and lighthouse will be used as an interpretive site to display and teach the history of lightkeeping.

Distant views are possible from the mainland on the east side of the harbor. Cruises from Boothbay Harbor pass this lighthouse; some trips originating at the Maine Maritime Museum include landing on the island. Scheduled trips to the island are planned from Boothbay Harbor at the start of the 2001 season.

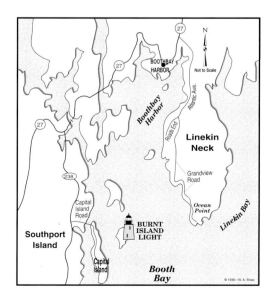

Directions: From U.S Rt. 1 take ME 27 south into Boothbay Harbor; all tour boats pass the light. To view the light from shore: Take ME 27 (Townsend) north to Union St. Turn right then right again at Atlantic Ave. Continue past Lobster Cove Rd. and Roads End Rd. to Grand View Rd. The lighthouse may be seen from several points along that road heading to the Spruce Point Inn. **Or..** Take Commercial St. (one way) to the Tugboat Inn; the light can be seen from the docks there.

Hendricks Head Light

The original light on the point of Southport Island on the east side of the mouth of the Sheepscot River was built atop a granite keeper's house in 1829. This structure was destroyed by fire in 1875 and replaced by the present lighthouse, a 39-foot square brick tower attached by a short walkway to the keeper's house. A pyramidal skeleton-type bell tower was added in 1890 and an oil house in 1895. In 1933 Hendricks Head Light was discontinued and sold to an individual. When electricity was brought to the house in 1951, the Coast Guard decided to reactivate the light in response to increased boating traffic in the area. The fifth-order Fresnel lens was replaced in 1979.

Two tales are associated with this station, one of an unusual rescue, another of an unidentified ghost. In the mid 19th century, following a March gale and shipwreck, the lightkeeper noticed a bundle floating toward shore and plucked it from the waves. The small package turned out to be an infant wrapped in a box between two feather mattresses for protection. The baby girl

survived the ordeal but the vessel vanished beneath the waves as wreckage began to wash ashore. There were no other survivors. Having recently buried their own daughter, the keeper and his wife adopted the baby and raised her at the lighthouse.

Another tale concerns a keeper whose tenure included the years between the first and second world wars. He reported the presence of an unknown woman walking in the area of the Southport post office; the postmaster also mentioned seeing the woman but neither had spoken to her. Her body was found the next day, weighted down with a flatiron. She was buried in Southport, her identity never known. Her ghostly figure has been reportedly seen walking the deserted beach in winter months, haunting the site where she apparently committed suicide.

The property remains privately owned and can be seen from the West Southport beach. Best views are available from excursion boats from Boothbay Harbor or Maine Maritime Museum.

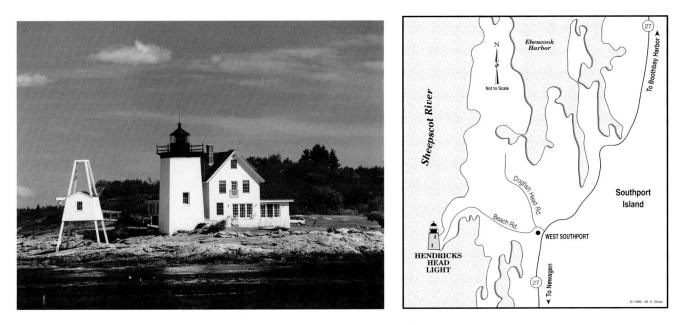

Directions: From U.S. Route 1, take ME 27 south into Boothbay Harbor. Continue on ME 27 to Southport Island. Bear right around a triangular intersection (Southport General Store on the right), then, as the road dips down, bear left at the "Beach Road" sign. Continue about 0.5 mile to the beach and parking area. Cruises from Boothbay Harbor and Maine Maritime Museum pass this light.

Ram Island Light

This light is located on Ram Island off Ocean Point on the eastern side of Boothbay Harbor. Built by order of President Chester A. Arthur in 1883, the brick lighthouse on granite base is similar to the towers at Marshall Point and Isle au Haut, and included a wooden walkway connecting the tower to the island. A Victorian keeper's house and fog bell tower also were built in 1883 and an oil house added in 1898.

The original aid to navigation on Ram Island was a lantern in the bow of a fisherman's anchored dory. Custom dictated that the last fisherman into the harbor each day would light the lantern, but this routine ended when the dory was wrecked in a storm. Another fisherman then moved the lantern to the island and tended the light. Shipwrecks continued however, as this light was not bright enough to warn vessels away from the rocks. For some years thereafter, Ram Island had no light and locals talked of ghosts guiding ships to safe passage. Tales include a sounding fog whistle (there was no signal on the island), a burning boat at night, gone without trace the following day, and a woman in white waving a lighted torch.

Ram Island Light was automated in 1965; the house was vandalized and the fourth-order Fresnel lens stolen in 1975. In 1977, the Coast Guard repaired the lighthouse and removed the walkway which had fallen into disrepair. The boathouse was destroyed by a winter storm in 1978.

Scheduled for demolition in 1983, the keeper's house was rescued by the Grand Banks Schooner Museum Trust, which leased the property and grounds. The Ram Island Preservation Society, an offshoot off the parent trust, has since restored the house; part-time caretakers now live on the island during the summer. The Grand Banks Schooner Museum is the restored *Sherman Zwicker* often on sojourn at the Maine Maritime Museum in Bath.

Lighthouse cruises from Maine Maritime Museum often include landing on the island. Some excursion boats from Boothbay Harbor pass this light as do the boats en route to Monhegan Island. The lighthouse also can be viewed in the distance from Ocean Point near Boothbay Harbor.

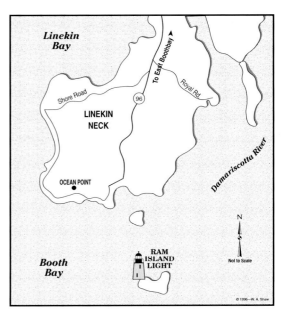

Directions: From U.S. 1 take ME 27 south to Boothbay Harbor. Then take ME 96 east and south to Ocean Point and follow the shoreline loop road. Along that road there are numerous points to view the lighthouse across Fisherman Island passage.

Seguin Island Light

Maine's second lighthouse was built in 1795 by order of President George Washington. Located at the mouth of the heavily travelled Kennebec River, two and one-half miles from Popham Beach, this light is the highest above water on the Maine coast. Although the tower at Seguin is not the tallest structure on the coast, the light is the highest due to its location on the island. At 186 feet above sea level, the light is visible from a distance of 40 miles in clear weather.

The original wooden tower was replaced by a stone structure in 1819 which was then rebuilt in 1857. The present 53-foot granite light tower was necessary to accommodate the installation of Maine's only first-order Fresnel lens. A duplex keeper's house also was added in 1857. In order to transport supplies up the steep quarter-mile climb to the lighthouse, a tramway system was installed with tracks from the boathouse to the keeper's dwelling. Because of heavy fog often in this area, Seguin has one of the most powerful foghorns made.

One of a variety of ghost stories associated with the lighthouse concerns a 19th century keeper's wife who played the same tune on the piano, over and over. The keeper was driven insane by the repetition, took an ax to the piano, then killed his wife and himself. Legend has it that the piano tune can still be heard drifting from the island on calm nights.

The light was automated in 1985; a group of concerned local citizens founded the Friends of Seguin Island in 1986. Although the Coast Guard maintains the light itself, the island and keeper's quarters are managed by the nonprofit group. By 1990 public contributions, grants from the Maine Historic Preservation Commission, National Park Service and matching fund programs made possible restoration of the keeper's quarters to accommodate summertime caretakers. In August of 1993 the Friends of Seguin opened a small museum in the lower two rooms on the north side of the keeper's house. Restoration, repair and maintenance of the grounds and buildings are ongoing efforts by this group.

Seguin light can be seen in the distance from the Popham Beach area and Maine Maritime Museum offers trips to the island during the summer. There is no dock or pier landing. Passengers are off-loaded into a skiff and taken to the beach; the climb to the lighthouse is fairly steep up a narrow path. Weather and sea conditions are extremely variable in this area and may preclude landing.

(Continued)

109

Seguin Island Light

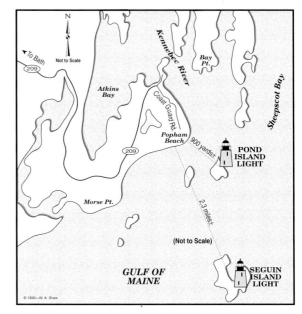

Directions: From U.S. Route 1 in Bath, take RT 209 to Popham Beach. Both Seguin Island and the nearer Pond Island light are visible in the distance.

* Maine Maritime Museum: From U.S. Route 1 in Bath, take the"Historic Bath"/Front St. exit, turning onto Washington St. Follow the signs past Bath Iron Works to the Museum (clearly marked): 243 Washington St., Bath, ME. 04530 (207) 443-6100 or (207) 443-1316.

Pond Island Light

Rocky, ten-acre Pond Island at the mouth of the Kennebec River, off Popham Beach, has no pond; the origin of the name is unknown. Soldiers were quartered on the island during the War of 1812 to prevent the British from entering the Kennebec and the island was a transfer point for steamer passengers in the 1820s.

The first stone lighthouse was built on the island in 1821, marking the east side entrance to the Kennebec River, about two miles northwest of Seguin Island. This structure lasted until 1855 when the present 20-foot brick tower was constructed and fitted with a fifth-order Fresnel lens. Pond Island light was automated in 1963 and all buildings except the lighthouse tower were destroyed by the Coast Guard. The U.S. Fish and Wildlife Service now manages the island as a bird refuge.

The light may be viewed distantly from the Popham Beach area. Closer views are available from tour boats in Boothbay Harbor and Bath's Maine Maritime Museum.

Directions: From U.S. Route 1 in Bath, ME., take ME 209 to Popham Beach. *Maine Maritime Museum-From U.S. Route 1 in Bath, take the "Historic Bath" exit. Turn onto Washington St and follow the signs past Bath Iron Works to the Museum (clearly marked), 243 Washington St.

Squirrel Point Light

Located on the southwest point of Arrowsic Island, this lighthouse is one of several aids to navigation built along the Kennebec River in 1898. The 25-foot wooden tower is similar to the lighthouses at Doubling Point and Perkins Island (both on the Kennebec). The keeper's house also was built in 1898, with the boathouse and oil house added a few years later; a fifth-order Fresnel lens was installed.

After being operated for a time by the keeper at the Kennebec River Light station, the Squirrel Point light was automated in 1979. The keeper's house is now privately owned. Cruises from Maine Maritime Museum in Bath and excursion boats from Boothbay Harbor pass this light; there is also a footpath to the lighthouse.

Original fifth-order lens used at Squirrel Point Light

Directions: The light may be seen distantly across the river from Phippsburg on ME 209. Turn left onto Parker Head Rd.; the light can be seen to the left directly across the river. Alternatively, from U.S. Route 1 just north of Bath, take RT 127 toward Arrowsic. Continue for about 4.5 miles; just before reaching the Georgetown-Arrowsic bridge, turn right onto Steen Road, then bear left onto Bald Head Road (dirt). This road ends after about 0.5 mile in a small parking area. From that area is a footpath to the lighthouse (about 3/4 mile). The path begins straight ahead from the parking area; listen for the sound of water and look for the shoreline. After crossing a small, wooden bridge the path through the woods to the lighthouse is marked with faint yellow blazes. Keep the water (Kennebec River) to your right on the way to the lighthouse and on your left when returning.

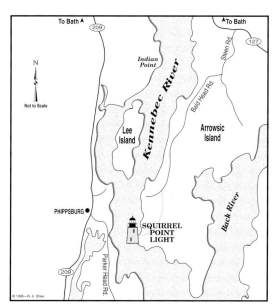

The Cuckholds Light

In 1892 a stone fog signal station and keeper's house were built on this small island less than a mile off the tip of Southport Island and the village of Newagen. But shipwrecks continued in the area of the Cuckholds, Boothbay Harbor became a major fishing port,and local mariners requested a lighthouse. Because the Cuckholds was too small to support a separate structure, a small light tower was added atop the original signal house in 1907. An attached two-story keeper's dwelling also was built. The light, one of the last built on the Maine coast, was named after a pair of treacherous ledges at the entrance to Boothbay Harbor. Apparently the Cuckholds refers to a point of land on the Thames River in England. The story goes that King John had an affair with the wife of a London man; to assuage the man's anger the king granted him the land on the Thames. It's then suggested that the Cuckholds in Maine may have been named by a transplanted Londoner.

The light was automated in 1975, the Fresnel lens removed and the property abandoned; a winter storm in 1978 swept away the keeper's house and other outbuildings. Many excursion boats from Boothbay Harbor pass light as do some trips from Maine Maritime Museum; distant views are possible from shore locations.

Directions: From U.S. Route 1, take ME 27 south into Boothbay Harbor. Continue on RT 27 to Southport Island to the Village of Newagen. At the post office ME 27 turns 90 degrees north into ME 238; bear southeast into a paved road with a "Town Landing" sign at the corner. Continue to a small parking area at the public pier. The lighthouse can be seen in the distance.

Perkins Island Light

In 1898 this 23-foot octagonal wooden tower was erected on seven-acre Perkins Island on the eastern side of the Kennebec River. A two-story keeper's house was built at the same time; the station is similar to the Doubling Point and Squirrel Point lights. The boathouse, bell tower and oil house were added in the early 1900s. The lighthouse originally had a fifth-order Fresnel lens.

Following automation in 1959 this lens was removed and a 250mm optic added; the fog bell also was removed. The property was turned over to the town of Georgetown in 1973 but little has been done to improve or maintain the grounds; the keeper's house and outbuildings are in disrepair. The light may be seen across the river from the village of Parker Head. Cruises from Maine Maritime Museum and Boothbay Harbor also pass the light.

In 2000 the American Lighthouse Foundation was given long-term lease to the tower and plans are underway for restoration. Volunteers have already begun restoration of the 1902 bell tower; it will be the original white when the project is complete.

Directions: From US Route 1, take High Street/RT 209 to Phippsburg. Turn left onto Parker Head Rd. This road follows the river into the village of Parker Head. The light can be seen distantly across the Kennebec River. An excursion boat from Maine Maritime Museum or Boothbay Harbor will offer the best views.

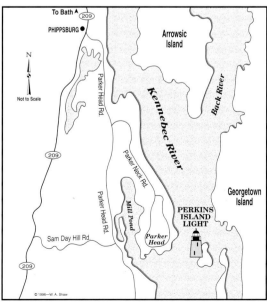

Kennebec River Range Lights

Several lighthouses were built in 1898 to aid mariners traveling along the Kennebec River toward the shipbuilding center of Bath. These lights (originally known as Doubling Point Range Lights) were established on Arrowsic Island in 1908; the two wooden towers are the only range lights in Maine. Straight alignment of the lights indicates to vessels the middle of the river channel on approach to Fiddler Reach, a sharp double bend in the river just beyond at Doubling Point.

The front range light is 21 feet high, the rear light 13 feet tall; the towers are 235 feet apart and each originally held a fifth-order Fresnel lens (both were removed in 1979). A wooden walkway connects the keeper's house and two towers. A boathouse was added in 1901 and an oil house in 1902. A bell tower in disrepair still stands between the Kennebec and Doubling point stations.

Front Light

Beginning in 1938, efforts were made to consolidate and automate the series of Kennebec River lighthouses. The keeper at the Kennebec station was given the additional duty of keeping Doubling Point Light, just around the bend in the river. Then in 1979, responsibility for the Kennebec and Doubling Point lights was assumed by the keeper at Squirrel Point Light. Finally, in 1981, the Coast Guard moved the keeper from Squirrel Point back to the Kennebec Station.

In 1982 the station was renamed Kennebec River Light Station and was the first to be tended by a woman resident keeper. The range lights were automated in 1990. A Coast Guard family now lives in the keeper's house, and the grounds are open to visitors.

Rear Light

All lighthouse trips from Maine Maritime Museum pass the range lights as do some boats from Boothbay Harbor.

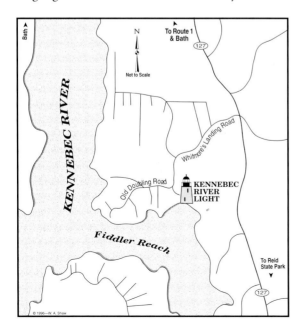

Directions: From U.S. Route 1 in Woolwich, turn south onto ME 127. After about 1.5 miles, just before the Arrowsic Town Hall, turn right onto Whitmore Landing Rd to Doubling Point Road (marked). At the first fork, turn left into Doubling Point Rd; bear left at the next fork and continue on the narrow lane to the lights. There is a boardwalk leading to the lighthouses. These lights are seen on Kennebec River trips from Boothbay Harbor or Maine Maritime Museum.

Doubling Point Light

Located at a sharp double bend in the Kennebec River, this lighthouse was built in 1898 on the northwest end of Arrowsic Island to guide mariners into Bath. Among the four Kennebec River lights, Doubling Point is the closest to the shipbuilding harbor. The wood octagonal tower is connected to the island by a wooden walkway and originally held a fifth-order Fresnel lens; a wood frame keeper's house, oil house and bell tower were built at the same time.

The keeper's house was sold to a private owner in 1934 and the lighthouse became the responsibility of the keeper at Doubling Point Range Lights up the river (also known as Kennebec River Range Lights). Following automation in 1979, the Fresnel lens was removed and the keeper at Squirrel Point Light assumed responsibility for monitoring the light. Finally, in 1981, the job of monitoring of all three lights (Doubling Point, Squirrel Point and the Kennebec River Range Lights) was given to the keeper at the Kennebec River station.

The lighthouse is accessible from the island and may be seen distantly from the shoreline in Bath. Frequent cruises from Maine Maritime Museum pass this light as do some excursion boats out of Boothbay Harbor.

Directions: From U.S. Route 1 in Woolwich, turn south onto ME 127. After about 1.5 miles, just before the Arrowsic Town Hall, turn right onto Whitmore Landing Rd to Doubling Point Road (marked). At the first fork, turn left into Doubling Point Rd. Continue straight on the narrow road to the light. Also, from U.S. Route 1 in Bath, take the High Street/ RT 209 exit to Phippsburg. The light may be seen across the river just a short distance south of Bath. Cruises from Maine Maritime Museum pass close by the light.

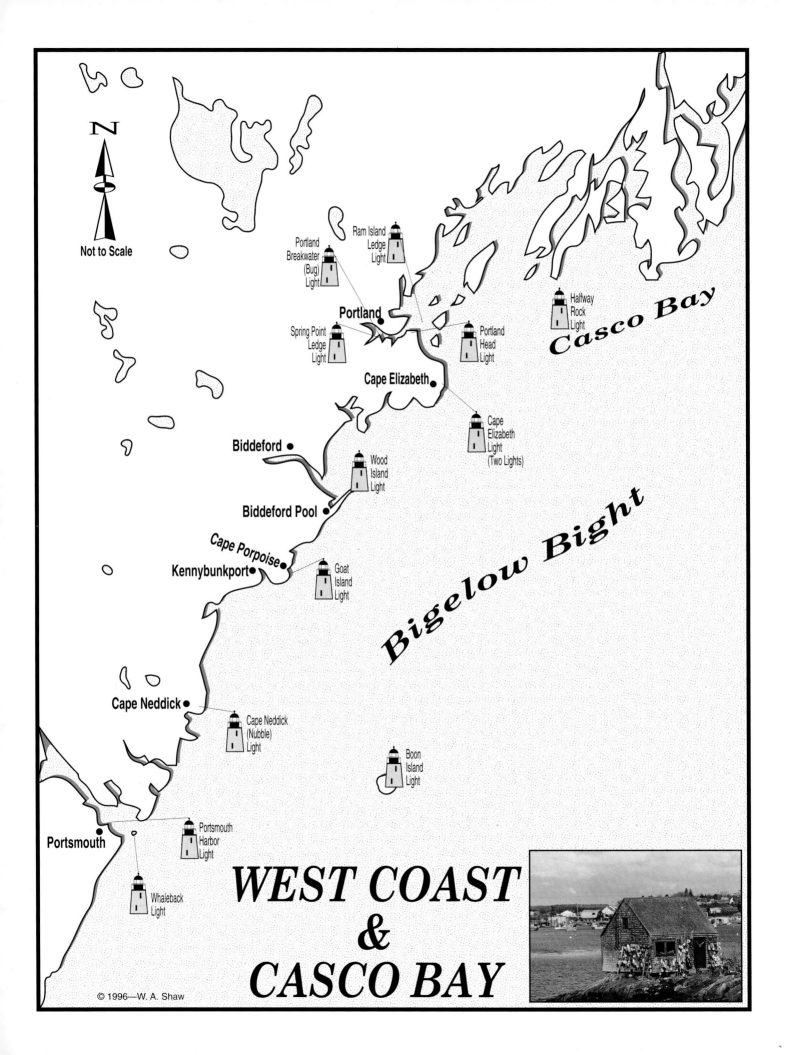

N

Not to Scale

Portland
Breakwater
(Bug)
Light

Ram Island
Ledge
Light

Halfway
Rock
Light

Casco Bay

Portland

Spring Point
Ledge
Light

Portland
Head
Light

Cape Elizabeth

Cape
Elizabeth
Light
(Two Lights)

Biddeford

Wood
Island
Light

Bigelow Bight

Biddeford Pool

Cape Porpoise

Kennybunkport

Goat
Island
Light

Cape Neddick

Cape Neddick
(Nubble)
Light

Boon
Island
Light

Portsmouth
Harbor
Light

Portsmouth

Whaleback
Light

WEST COAST
&
CASCO BAY

Halfway Rock Light

Named because it is halfway between Cape Elizabeth and Cape Small in Casco Bay, this barren three-acre rocky ledge is located about 11 miles northeast of Portland Head in a busy shipping lane. Treacherous ledges are found around Halfway Rock. Construction of the light was begun in 1870 but bad weather and funding glitches delayed completion of the 66-foot granite tower until 1871. The original tower held a third-order Fresnel lens and served as quarters for the keepers as well. A 43-foot bell tower was added near the lighthouse in 1887, with a raised walkway connecting the lighthouse and bell tower. In 1888 a boathouse was built with keeper's quarters in the upper story.

In 1960 a keeper's house was built, a new boathouse added and helicopter landing pad constructed in 1961. The station suffered substantial damange in storms of 1962 and 1972. The '72 storm washed away outbuildings and equipment and helicopter evacuation of the crew was required. The light was automated in 1975. All buildings at Halfway Rock except the lighthouse tower and entryway have since succumbed to storms. Although the light can be seen distantly from the end of Orr's/Bailey Island, best views are by boat.

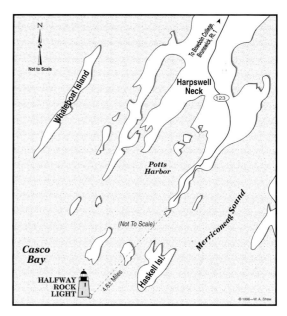

Directions: Although on a clear day this light may be seen in the distance from aboard a Casco Bay Cruise boat, these excursions do not allow for close views or photography. A custom boat charter may be arranged out of Harpswell. A distant view is possible by taking RT 24 south from Brunswick at the Cook's Corner intersection to Orr's & Bailey Islands. Continue to a small parking area and gift shop at the end of the road.

Spring Point Ledge Light

This lighthouse marks the dangerous ledge on the west side of the main shipping channel into Portland Harbor. Many vessels ran aground here before a group of steamship companies convinced the government to locate a lighthouse on the ledge in 1891. However, Congress failed to allocate funds until 1896 when construction began. Setbacks in construction, including storms and disputes about materials, delayed completion until May 1897. Built on a cylindrical cast-iron caisson, the lighthouses is a typical "sparkplug" style of the period, but unlike many such structures, the tower is constructed of brick rather than cast iron.

The lighthouse includes four levels, including a keeper's office, watchroom, and two levels for living quarters. A fifth-order Fresnel lens was installed and a fog bell hung on the side of the tower. The light was electrified and automated in 1934; in 1951 the 900-foot breakwater was constructed, joining the lighthouse with the mainland. Restoration of the interior tower is ongoing; period furnishings will be included to replicate the keeper's living quarters. Tours of the interior are offered during open houses scheduled periodically throughout the year.

The lighthouse is easily accessible; the Portland Harbor Museum is located in the adjacent to the Southern Maine Technical College campus. Excursion boats from Portland pass near this light.

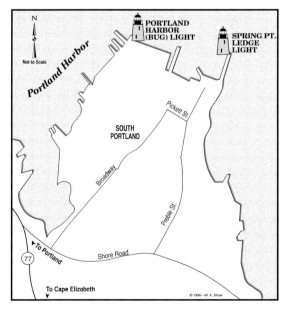

Directions: From ME 77 in Portland, continue over the bridge to So. Portland onto Broadway. Follow Broadway straight, to its end; turn right onto Pickett St. and follow it to the end. Turn left onto Fort Road which ends at Fort Preble (now Southern Maine Technical College) and a parking area. The light and breakwater are immediately ahead just to the right.

Portland Breakwater(Bug) Light

A 2,500-foot breakwater and lighthouse on the south side of the entrance to Portland Harbor were planned after a storm in November 1831 severely damaged the area. Although construction began in 1836, lack of funds caused delay but in 1855 a small octagonal wooden tower with a sixth-order Fresnel lens was in operation.

In the early 1870s the breakwater was extended approximately 200 feet and a new lighthouse built at the end. Known locally as "Bug Light", the new lighthouse included Greek architectural elements. The design of the cast-iron tower is unique: petite, with Corinthian columns created to resemble a 4th century (B.C.) Greek monument. A wooden keeper's

house was built adjacent to the lighthouse in 1889. In 1934 the light was electrified, the keeper's house removed and the light tended by the keeper at Spring Point Ledge Light. As shipyards expanded into the harbor to accommodate World War II shipbuilding, the breakwater progressively shortened until the lighthouse stood only 100 feet from shore, making it obsolete. The light was extinguished in 1942, declared surplus property soon after, and sold to private ownership. The property was later donated to the city of Portland. In 1989, after long standing unattended, repair and restoration were accomplished with money from federal, state and local organizations.

C.1921

Directions: Take RT 77 from South Portland to Broadway.
Turn east on Broadway and continue to Pickett Street. Turn left onto Pickett Street; follow that road around the warehouses then bear right to the parking area. Parking also is possible in the South Portland landing lot, free if viewing the light. To the right is a walkway to the light. Tour boats from Portland also offer good views. (*Note map previous page*)

Ram Island Ledge Light

This light sits on jagged rocks which extend a quarter mile from Ram Island at the northern entrance to Portland Harbor. At high tide the ledges are entirely covered. In 1855 an iron spindle was placed on the ledge as a navigational aid and a larger, 50-foot wooden tripod erected in 1873. While helpful in clear weather, the markers became virtually invisible in bad conditions. Shipwrecks were frequent, but the grounding of the 400-foot transatlantic steamer *California* in a snowstorm finally convinced the government that a lighthouse was needed. Congress appropriated funds for the construction in 1902; a granite tower was planned.

Work began in 1903 but because the ledge was submerged much of the time, construction could take place only at low tide. The granite blocks (which make the tower appear older than it is) came from Vinalhaven, were numbered to indicate position, then ferried to the ledge. In 1904 the tower was completed, with a 26,000-pound lantern placed and

third-order Fresnel lens installed. The lighthouse was then 90 feet tall, with the light 77 feet above sea level, first lighted in January 1905.

Three lightkeepers were assigned to Ram Island Ledge, each working two-week shifts, followed by a week shore leave. Living quarters were inside the tower. In 1958 the light was electrified, then automated in 1959; keepers at Portland Head Light monitored the ledge station. The light is visible offshore from Ft. Williams Park in Cape Elizabeth and from points along the shore; some tour boats from Portland pass the light.

Directions: From U.S. Route 1 in Portland, take the ME 77 exit (Congress St) and follow that route through Portland, past the harbor to South Portland, then into Cape Elizabeth. Turn left at the "Portland Head Light" sign onto Shore Road; continue to Fort Williams State Park and Portland Head Light. The Casco Bay cruises and harbor trips offer distant views of this light; a custom boat charter is the only way to get close photographs.

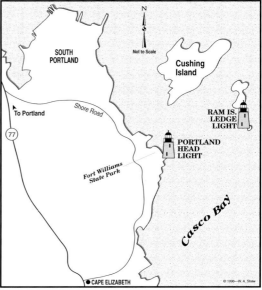

Portland Head Light

The patriarch of Maine's lighthouses marks the state's busiest harbor, boasting a combination of historic significance and beauty which make it possibly the most visited, photographed and painted lighthouse in the United States. The setting particularly inspired Henry Wadsworth Longfellow, who found the tranquil beauty of the lighthouse well suited to writing poetry.

Maine was part of the Massachusetts Bay Colony in the 18th century and Portland(known as Falmouth until 1786), had become one of the busiest ports in America by the late 1700s. There were no lighthouses in Maine when, in 1784, merchants petitioned the Massachusetts government for a light to mark the entrance to Portland Harbor. John Hancock was then governor of the Bay Colony and authorized construction. Delayed by insufficient funds, construction didn't begin until 1790, with the original plan for a 58-foot tower revised to 72 feet. President George Washington appointed the first keeper, Captain Joseph Greenleaf.

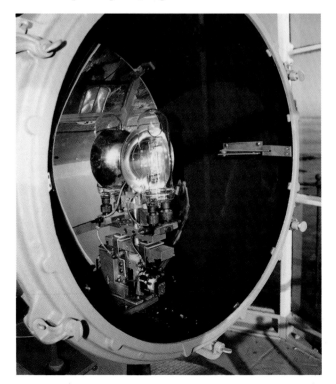

Repairs were made to the station in 1810, with an outdoor oil shed added. In 1813 a new lantern and system of lamps and reflectors designed by Winslow Lewis was installed; a new keeper's house was built in 1816. A fourth-order Fresnel lens replaced the lamps and reflectors in 1855 and a bell tower was added at that time.

Following the wreck of the Liverpool vessel *Bohemian* in which 40 immigrants died, the tower was raised 20 feet and a second-order Fresnel lens installed. However, with the completion of Halfway Rock Light in 1871, Portland Head Light was considered less important. In 1833, the tower was shortened 20 feet and the weaker fourth-order Fresnel lens returned. The former tower height and second order lens were restored in 1835 following mariners' complaints.

(Continued)

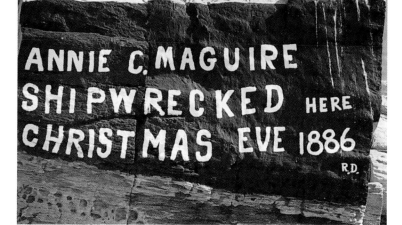

Portland Head Light

A rock near the lighthouse marks the spot where, on Christmas Eve 1886, the British bark *Annie C. Maguire* ran shore at Portland Head. The keepers helped all on board to shore safely but the ship was destroyed by a storm on New Year's Day 1887.

A new keeper's house was built in 1891; the station has changed little since then except for replacement of the Fresnel lens with a modern optic. The light was automated in August, 1989. Renovation of the keeper's quarters was accomplished in 1990 to create a museum, dedicated in 1992, now operated by the Town of Cape Elizabeth. Portland Head Light is adjacent to Fort Williams State Park.

"Sail on, Sail on ye stately ships;
And with you floating bridge the ocean span.
Be mine to guard this light from all eclipse
Be yours to bring man near unto man"

--Henry Wadsworth Longfellow

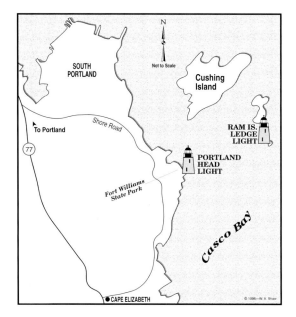

Directions: From I-95, 295, or U.S. 1, take ME 77 to Cape Elizabeth (clearly marked). Turn east onto Shore Road and follow that road to Fort Williams State Park (several "Portland Head Light" signs direct you). The light can also be photographed from a tour boat out of Portland.

Cape Elizabeth Light (Two Lights)

The entrance to Portland Harbor was marked with a 50-foot stone black and white pyramidal day beacon placed in 1811 at the site of the present Cape Elizabeth Light, about eight miles southeast of Portland. Captain John Smith had named the area in honor of Princess Elizabeth, daughter of King James I and Queen Anne of Denmark.

In 1827 the initial stone marker was demolished when the first pair of lighthouses was built. The east light was located at the site of the old marker, with the inner light directly to the west. Mariners aligned the two 65-foot rubblestone towers in order to position a vessel properly in the channel into Portland Harbor. The west light was discontinued in 1855 by the Lighthouse Board. Subsequently, local fishermen and lobstermen protested the inactivation of the light, whereupon it was reestablished in 1855. Fresnel lenses were installed in both towers in 1855 and in 1865 both were repainted. To aid in daytime recognition, four horizontal red bands were painted on the east tower and a single, broad vertical red stripe added to the west tower.

In 1874 the original Two Lights were replaced by new 67-foot cast-iron towers 300 yards apart, with second order Fresnel lenses installed in each. The west light was briefly discontinued in 1882, but was relit after complaints that the east light was easily confused with nearby Wood Island Light.

For a time both towers were painted brown, but have been white since 1902. In 1924 the government mandated that all twin light stations be reduced to single lights; the west light at Cape Elizabeth was then permanently discontinued. Subsequently, the property was sold to several private owners, renovated and restored.

Cape Elizabeth Light (Two Lights)

The remaining lighthouse was automated in 1963 and the 1,800-pound Fresnel lens removed in 1994. Visible for 27 nautical miles, the active, functioning east tower is the most powerful on the New England coast at four million candle power. The 1878 Victorian keeper's house is now privately owned. The assistant keeper's house was incorporated into a new home. Cape Elizabeth Light was the subject of two Edward Hopper paintings, one of which was reproduced on a 1970 issue postage stamp commemorating Maine's 150th anniversary. Recently a significant addition to the former keeper's house was undertaken.

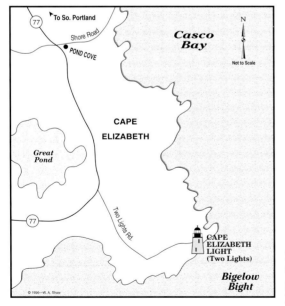

Directions: From Portland/South Portland, take RT 77 to Cape Elizabeth. Continue about four miles, then bear left onto Two Lights Road (Two Lights State Park is to the right). Continue for about 1.5 miles, turning left at Two Lights Terrace; the light and keeper's house (private property) are on a knoll at the end of the road. The inactive tower is to the left shortly after turning onto Two Lights Terrace. The active lighthouse also may be photographed from a park area at the end of Two Lights Road.

Wood Island Light

At the mouth of the Saco River off the village of Biddeford Pool, Wood Island Light was built in 1808 to guide mariners into Wood Island Harbor. The 47-foot rubblestone tower is the original, making it Maine's oldest lighthouse tower. A new keeper's house was added in 1858 and a fourth-order Fresnel lens installed. The light's lantern was removed in 1972

Old Orchard, Wood Island Light.

and a rotating aerobeacon installed. Complaints about the "headless" lighthouse prompted return of the lantern and installation of a smaller lens at the time of automation in 1986.

Legend says that this island is haunted by the ghost of a murder victim. The tale involves a lobsterman/ sometime-policeman who lived on the island. Thought of as a gentle giant, the man's life proceeded peacefully until a younger man settled on Wood Island. Soon after, the lobsterman found his new neighbor wandering the island, drunk after a heavy session in a mainland bar. The young man brandished a rifle and fired at the lobsterman, mortally wounding him. When the lighthouse keeper found the young man wandering aimlessly, he advised the man surrender to authorities. Instead, the young man returned to his squatter's shack and shot himself in the head. Strange events on Wood Island over the years have been attributed to the ghost of the murdered lobsterman, haunting the area still.

Twenty eight of the island's 35 acres were deeded to the Maine Audubon Society in 1970. The lighthouse can be seen distantly from a trail along the shore in Biddeford Pool but is best seen by boat.

Directions: From ME 9 between Cape Porpoise and Biddeford, turn south onto ME 208. Alternatively, from US 1, take ME 111 into Biddeford toward Biddeford Pool. Turn south onto ME 208. Bear left at a "T" intersection, continuing on ME 208 to Biddeford Pool. Pass the firestation and continue about 0.5 mile— the road makes a right angle to follow the shoreline. Just before that turn there is a gate and a path to a well-marked footpath(Audubon Trail next to the golf course) with the lighthouse visible shortly ahead across the inlet.

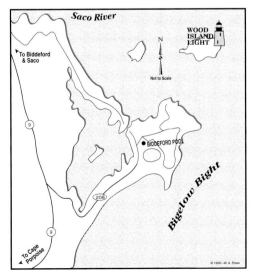

Goat Island Light

Established in 1834 to guide mariners into the sheltered harbor at Cape Porpoise, the lighthouse is located at the southwest end of Goat Island. In 1860 the 20-foot stone tower and keeper's house were rebuilt and a fifth-order Fresnel lens installed. The present 25-foot brick structure was built sometime between 1880-1890 and connected to the 1-1/2 story house by covered walkway. A boathouse was added in 1905 and oil house in 1907.

The Coast Guard planned to automate the light in 1976 but the towns of Biddeford and Kennebunkport successfully petitioned for a keeper on the island to prevent vandalism. Notable for being Maine's last manned light station, Goat Island became the final Maine lighthouse to be automated in 1990. At that time, the Fresnel lens also was replaced. The station was used as a security post when former President George Bush was in residence at Walker's Point in Kennebunkport. Goat Island was leased to the Kennebunkport Conservation Trust in 1992. Plans call for reconstruction of the covered walkway destroyed in the Blizzard of 1978. The lighthouse can be seen from the wharf in Cape Porpoise.

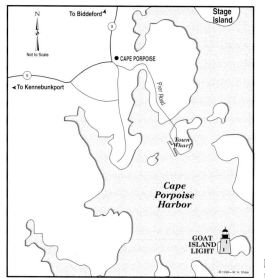

Directions: From I-95 take the Kennebunkport exit, follow ME 35 into Kennebunk. Take ME 9A south to Kennebunkport (or from US 1. take RT 9A also). Route 9A becomes RT 9; continue through Kennebunkport to Cape Porpoise Center. Where ME 9 makes a 90-degree turn left, instead **bear right** onto Pier Road which ends at the wharf. The light is offshore to the southeast. Better photographs are possible from a tour boat out of Kennebunkport.

Boon Island Light

Standing on a small, rocky, barren island about 6.5 miles southeast of Cape Neddick, this light is clearly one of the most isolated. Severe storms, typical of this area, have swept away numerous light towers on this ledge. The first 50 foot wooden tower was established in 1800 but the flimsy wooden structure was destroyed by a winter storm in 1804; it was replaced with a stone tower the following summer. President James Madison authorized a new lighthouse in 1812 but storms again destroyed the light in 1831. Finally, the Lighthouse Board allowed that a much more sound, substantial structure was required. In 1852 the present light tower was constructed and, at 133 feet, is the tallest in New England, measuring 25 feet in diameter at the base, 12 feet wide at the top.

Tales and legends involving the island are numerous but the most well-known incident was the wreck of the British ship *Nottingham Galley* in December 1710. Survivors struggled to stay alive for three weeks, finally resorting to cannibalism. It's said that after this disaster local fishermen began leaving barrels of provisions (a "boon") in case of future wrecks. Legends also tell of a keeper's wife driven mad after her husband's death on the island, of a keeper who left the island for food, later found wandering aimlessly hundreds of miles away and of marooned keepers saved by a the crew of a passing schooner who retrieved their plea for help set adrift in a bottle.

This island is continually pounded by the sea; the Blizzard of 1978 destroyed the keeper's house and outbuildings as five feet of water inundated the station. During that storm granite boulders were tossed about as if they were pebbles. The two keepers, having taken refuge in the tower, were rescued by helicopter the following day. Shortly after this storm Boon Island Light was automated; the second-order Fresnel lens was removed in 1993 and replaced by a modern solar-powered optic. The original Fresnel lens is on display at the Kittery Historical & Naval Museum located next to the Town Hall.

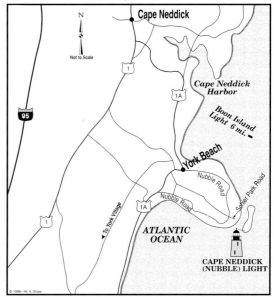

Directions: From I-95 or U.S. Route 1 in York, take U.S. 1A to York Beach, continuing to Nubble Road (marked with a small "Nubble Light" sign). Follow this road to Sohier Park and the parking area. The light is visible in the distance. To view the lens, the museum is at the intersection of Rogers Rd. Extension and US Route 1 in Kittery, ME.

Cape Neddick (Nubble) Light

A lighthouse on the small, rocky island (the nubble) off the eastern point of Cape Neddick, had been recommended by local mariners since 1807, but it wasn't until seventy years later that the lighthouse was established. The 41-foot cast-iron tower was authorized by President Rutherford B. Hayes and first illuminated in July 1879. Although initially painted red, the tower has been white since 1902. The distinctive red oil house was built in 1902 and the walkway connecting the keeper's house and tower added in 1911. The station originally had a fog bell and bell tower; this structure was razed in 1961. An 1891 fourth-order lens, although not the original, still is in use. A bucet suspended on a line across the channel

was used to transport supplies to the station; the conveyance is similarly used today for maintenance equipment. Unique to this light tower are the miniature cast-iron lighthouses atop the posts on the railing surrounding the lantern room. Also distinguishing Cape Neddick Light was a past feline resident who, at 19 pounds, reportedly attracted as many interested tourists as did the lighthouse itself. The cat allegedly was the best mouser in Maine, regularly swimming the channel to visit briefly with mainland friends, then returning to the lighthouse to deal with the mice.

Cape Neddick Light was automated in 1987; the Town of York now manages the surrounding property, having received more than 300 unsolicited offers from people wanting to be live-in caretakers. Some restoration work has been done with an 1989 grant from the Maine Historic Preservation Committee. Two small second story windows were replaced with one large window to restore the original appearance of the house.

The lighthouse and grounds are among the most appealing and photographed in the world, with an estimated 250,00 visitors annually. In 1977 NASA sent Voyager II into space with items aboard designed to teach extraterrestrial civilizations about our planet; a picture of the Nubble Light was among the images included.

The Town of York sponsors periodic excursions to the island during the summer; visitors are able to tour the tower and keeper's house.

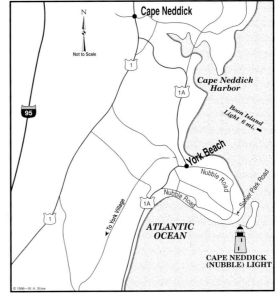

Directions: From I-95 or U.S. Route 1 in York, take U.S. 1A to York Beach, continuing to Nubble Road (marked with a small "Nubble Light" sign). Follow this road to Sohier Park and the parking area.

Portsmouth Harbor Light

A lantern on a pole was the first "lighthouse" established in 1771 at Ft. William and Mary, a British stronghold on Newcastle Island guarding Portsmouth Harbor. The first overt act of the Revolutionary War occurred in the area in December 1774. After learning of British plans to strengthen the fort, Paul Revere rode to Portsmouth from Boston with the news. Forewarned, the colonists overpowered the fort and made off with supplies.

A more permanent tower was built during the period 1782-1784, making it one of America's twelve colonial lighthouses. Following transfer of the property to the federal government, President George Washington is said to have visited the lighthouse.

In 1804 a new octagonal wooden tower was constructed and replaced in 1877 with a new 48-foot cast-iron tower; a fourth-order Fresnel lens was installed. The fortifications on Newcastle Island, now attached by causeway to the mainland, became known as Ft. Constitution. Portsmouth Harbor Light was automated in 1960 and is part of the Ft. Constitution Historic Site, adjacent to an active Coast Guard Station. Recently the Coast Guard restored the tower and the lighthouse is now licensed to the American Lighthouse Foundation which will oversee care of the site.

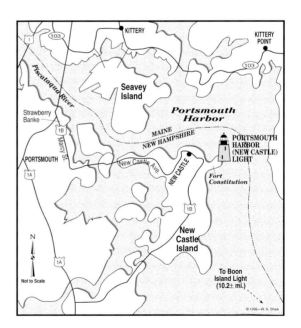

Directions: From I-95 or U.S. Route 1, take the waterfront exit and/or follow the signs to the Strawberry Banke area. Follow Marcy Street (RT 1B) through this area toward Newcastle; the road becomes New Castle Avenue. Continue on 1B into Newcastle to Wentworth Avenue. Turn left (Ft. Constitution Historic Site sign), then bear right to the parking area. The light can also be seen in the distance from Ft. McClary in Kittery, Maine.

Whaleback Light

Located at the northeast side of Portsmouth Harbor at the entrance to the Piscataqua River, this lighthouse is in Maine waters although guarding the entrance to the New Hampshire harbor. In 1829 President Andrew Jackson authorized construction of a 48-foot stone tower on the partially submerged ledge; construction was completed in 1831. A fourth-order Fresnel lens was installed in 1855 and fog bell added in 1859.

That light lasted almost 40 years despite the combination of faulty initial construction and repeated severe storms. By 1868 storm damage was irreparable and in 1872 a new 75-foot tower was built of granite blocks dovetailed together in similar fashion to Minots Ledge Light in Massachusetts and Eddystone Light in England. Upon completion of the new lighthouse, the old structure was cut down and used as signal house for a new fog trumpet. Part of the base of the old tower still remains.

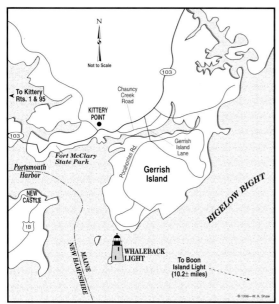

The light was automated in 1964 and the Fresnel lens replaced with a modern optic. The lighthouse can be seen from Ft. Foster, Ft. Constitution and points along the shore. Excursion boats from Portsmouth also pass the light.

Portsmouth, N.H., Whaleback Light, Portsmouth Harbor

Directions: From I-95 or U.S. Route 1 in Kittery, take ME 103 east. Continue on ME 103 past the entrance to the Portsmouth Naval Shipyard and the entrance to Ft. McClary. Pass the intersection with Hoyts Island Road, bear right to Chauncy Creek Road, then right again at Gerrish Island Lane. Cross over the bridge and bear right at Pocahontas Road to the park entrance. **Or:** From I-95 or U.S. Route 1, take the waterfront exit and follow the signs to Strawberry Banke area. Follow Marcy St. (RT 1B) toward Newcastle; the road becomes NewCastle Ave. Continue on 1B to NewCastle to Wentworth Ave. Turn left (Ft. Constitution Historic Site sign), then bear right to parking area.

White Island Light (Isles of Shoals)

White Island is one of nine windswept islands nine miles east of the mouth of the Piscataqua River. First known as the Smythes Isles (discovered by Captain John Smith in 1614), they were renamed by fisherman for plentiful schools, or shoals, of fish found in the area. A 17th-century land grant allotted the southern four islands to New Hampshire, the remainder to Maine.

The first Isles of Shoals lighthouse was an 87-foot stone tower established in 1821. White Island's second light, erected in 1859, remains in operation. The tower is a 58-foot cylindrical brick tower with walls two feet thick. This station was automated in 1987 and subsequently converted to solar power. Severe storms in the fall of 1992 destroyed the fog signal, covered walkways, and other equipment and outbuildings.

Nothing was done to replace any of the structures and in 1993 the light station was deeded to the State of New Hampshire. Renovations have since been undertaken. Excursion boats from Portsmouth will go to the Isles of Shoals, but not all go by White Island for close views of the lighthouse.

Directions: Coming into Portsmouth from any route, follow signs to the waterfront; some of the cruise boats go past this light and include Boon Island, Whaleback and Portsmouth Harbor lights.

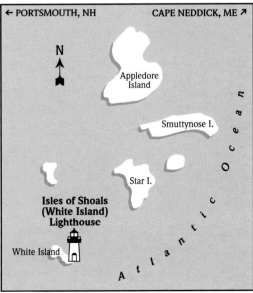

Maine's Lost Lighthouses

Avery Rock Light

President Ulysses S. Grant authorized construction of this light in 1874. Because the town of Machias had at that time developed into a major lumber port, location of a lighthouse at the south end of Machias Bay, about three miles from the mainland, was warranted to guide ships safely into the harbor. The square tower was built atop the brick keeper's house with a fifth order Fresnel lens was installed. An oil house and bell tower were built next to the dwelling. Duty at this station was not sought after due to the isolation but keeper's were permitted to bring their families with them nonetheless.

After numerous construction delays resulting from difficulty landing on the rock, the light was first illuminated in October 1875. A new fourth order lens was installed in 1902. Following destruction of the lighthouse by a storm in 1946, an automatic flashing buoy was placed 100 yards from the original site.

Crabtree Ledge Light

First lit in January 1890, this lighthouse was located to mark Crabtree Ledge about a mile off Hancock Point in Frenchman Bay. Passenger steamers bound for the railroad terminus at Hancock Point and ships carrying lumber and granite into the Taunton River were guided by this light.

The typical "sparkplug" style cast-iron structure contained a fifth order Fresnel lens which was visible for approximately 12nm; a bell was installed in 1891. The 37-foot iron tower originally was painted brown, but changed to white in 1903. After discontinuation in 1934, the light was sold to private ownership and subsequently collapsed into the bay during a winter storm.

St. Croix River Light

Photo: Coast Guard Archives

Located on Dochet Island, near Calais, Maine and the border with New Brunswick, Canada, this was one of the most remote lightstations in the country. The white frame keeper's house with lantern on top was built in 1857 to mark the entrance to the St. Croix River which was then a busy commercial waterway. Following discontinuation in 1957, the lighthouse stood abandoned on the island and fell victim to vandalism. In 1976 a group of juveniles hiding out on the island lit a fire to keep warm. The dry wood walls were ignited by a spark and the entire structure was rapidly engulfed in flames. Although the young people escaped the fire, they were apprehended by the authorities after destroying the historic lighthouse.

Fort Popham Light

Built in 1862, Fort Popham was one of many started in the early days of the Civil War but never completed. The light there, established in October 1899, was on an iron spindle next to the fort. A fog bell tower, foot bridge and plank walk to the shore were built in 1903 and the light moved to the tower. A keeper's house, similar in structure to that at Isle au Haut, was added in 1909. Records suggest the light was relocated to the top of the fort in 1949, the bell tower and lighthouse demolished after damage by lightning. The fate of the keeper's house is unknown.

Scenic/Tour Boat and Charter Information

Bold Coast and Downeast Coast Lights

*Andy Patterson, Bold Coast Charter Co., P.O. Box 364, Cutler, ME. 04626 (207) 259-4484. Although trips on the *Barbara Frost* to Machias Seal Island to view the puffins are his specialty, arrangements can be made for a trip to view the three lights in the area (Little River, Machias Seal Is., Libby Is.)

*Barna & John Norton , RR 01- 990, Jonesport, ME. 04649 (207)-497-5933. Trips to Machias Seal Is. to view puffins—Libby Is.light seen on the way. Area lighthouse trips arranged on request.

Air charter: Acadia Air, Hancock County/Bar Harbor Airport: Located in Trenton, Me. off ME 3. Only single engine planes available for local lighthouses, but they will arrange for flights to outermost lights. (207-667-5534).

Mt. Desert Area Lights

*Whale-watching trips out of Bar Harbor *may* head to feeding grounds in the Mt. Desert Rock area; Egg Rock Light may be seen on the way out. However, because the route is determined by location of the whales, close views of Mt. Desert Rock light cannot always be guaranteed. Puffin trips go to Petit Manan. *Acadian Whale Watcher* (207) 288-9794, (207) 288-9776, or 1-800-421-3307

* Northeast Harbor: Ferry and mail boat service to Cranberry Isles (*Sea Queen, Double B)* —Beal & Bunker, Inc. P.O. Box 33, Cranberry Isles, ME. 04625 (207) 244-3575. Passes Bear Island Light.
     Wes Shaw, MDI Water Taxi (Northeast Harbor)—P.O. Box 18, Mt. Desert, ME. (207) 244-7312. Specializes in custom trips for photography and is able, weather and seas permitting, to take a skiff for landing at offshore lights.

*Southwest Harbor: Ferry to Cranberry Isles (June-September)—Cranberry Cove Boating Co. (*Island Queen)*. (207) 244-5882. Trips to Baker Island.

Air Charters: *Acadia Air, Hancock Co./ Bar Harbor Airport, (Just off RT 3 in Trenton) (207)-667-5534.

Eggemoggin Reach and Penobscot Bay Lights

*The Elms Bed & Breakfast, Ted & Jo Panayotoff, 84 Elm St., Camden, ME 04843 (1-800-755-ELMS). The owners are lighthouse buffs and the inn's decor features lighthouse memorabilia of all sorts. A variety of specialty trips are offered by the inn throughout the season, featuring cruises to offshore lights in Penobscot Bay, the Fox Islands Thorofare, Eggemoggin Reach and Muscle Ridge Channel. Call for brochure and schedule.These trips aboard the *Lively Lady Too* are geared for photographers; Captain Alan Philbrick (207-236-6672) gives excellent close views of all lights.

*The Eagle Island mailboat out of Sunset, ME., Robert Quinn (207) 348-2817. Take RT 15 into Deer Isle and turn right at the post office (marked with a "Sunset" sign), bear right again at Pressey Village Road (0.5mile), then left onto Dunham Point Road. Continue on to Sylvester Cove (about 3.2 miles from the post office)

*To Isle au Haut (from Stonington, ME.) Mailboat/Ferry: *Miss Lizzie* makes scheduled trips to the town landing, about 0.8-1mile from the light; passengers going to the Keeper's House Bed & Breakfast are disembarked at the inn's private landing at Robinson Point. During the summer *The Mink* (June-Labor Day) takes visitors to Acadia National Park (Duck Harbor). *Miss Lizzie* daily June-September or by special arrangement. Isle au Haut Company, Herbert & George Aldrich (207) 367-5193 days, (207) 367-2355(evenings). The *Palmer Day* cruises along the coastline of Isle au Haut for five miles. (207)-367-2207.
* The *Betselma*, Penobscot Bay Cruises (Camden and Rockport Harbors), Camden Public Landing. (207) 236-2101. One & two-hour cruises to view Curtis, Indian and/or Grindle Point Light(s)
*Schooner/windjammer day cruises out of Camden, Rockport and Rockland

Air Charters: * Penobscot Air, Knox Co. Airport, Owl's Head, ME. (207) 596-6211. (Just off RT 3 in Trenton) * Ace Aviation, P.O. Box 457, Belfast, ME. (207)338-2970. (Just off Route 1 in Belfast-clearly marked)

Midcoast, Kennebec & Boothbay Area Lights

*The Elms Bed & Breakfast, Ted & Jo Panayotoff, 84 Elm St., Camden, ME . 04843 (1-800 755- ELMS). The owners are lighthouse buffs and the inn's decor features lighthouse memorabilia of all sorts. A variety of specialty trips are offered by the inn throughout the season, featuring cruises to offshore lights in Penobscot Bay, the Fox Islands Thorofare, Eggemoggin Reach and Muscle Ridge Channel. Call for brochure and schedule.These trips aboard the *Lively Lady Too* are geared for photographers; Captain Alan Philbrick (207) 236-6672 gives excellent close views of all lights.

Midcoast, Kennebec & Boothbay Area Lights (con't)

Monhegan Island: Reached by boat from either Boothbay Harbor, New Harbor or Port Clyde:

        *Port Clyde: From U.S. Route 1 in Thomaston, turn south onto ME 131 and follow this road through St. George and Tenant's Harbor into Port Clyde. The passenger ferry and mailboat from Port Clyde (*Elizabeth Ann , Laura B)* provide service to the island year 'round. (207) 372-8848.

        *New Harbor: From U.S. Route 1 in Waldoboro, take ME 32 to New Harbor. The *Hardy III* departs from Shaw's Fish & Lobster Wharf Restaurant. P.O. Box 326, New Harbor, ME. 04554 (207) 677-2026. Operates Memorial Day to mid-September

        *Boothbay Harbor trips (From US 1, take ME 27 south into Boothbay Harbor)

    Capt. Fish's Boat Trips, Pier 1, (207) 633-3244 or (207) 633-2626 or Balmy Days Cruises, *Balmy Days II,* Pier 8 P.O. Box 535, Boothbay Harbor, ME. 04538 (207) 633-2284. Operates mid-May to mid-October.

* The passenger ferry and/or mailboat to Monhegan from Pt. Clyde passes Marshall Point Light. (*Elizabeth Anne or Laura B)*

*Maine Maritime Museum - 243 Washington St., Bath, ME. 04530 (207) 443-6100 or (207) 443-1316. From U.S. Route 1 in Bath, take the "Historic Bath" or "Front Street" exit, turning onto Washington St. Follow the signs to the Museum.

Air Charters: **Penobscot Air,** Knox Co. Airport, Owl's Head, ME. (207) 596-6211.

Casco Bay & West Coast Lights

*Eagle Tours, 19 Pilot Rd., Cape Elizabeth, ME. 04107 (207) 774-6498 ***Bay View Cruises,** 184 Commercial St., Portland, ME. 04101 (207) 761-0496 ***Longfellow Cruise Line,** One Long Wharf, Portland, ME. 04101 (207) 774-3578 ***Casco Bay Lines,** P.O. Box 4656, Portland, ME. 04112 (207) 744-7871 ***Cape Arundel Cruises** (*Elizabeth 2),* P.O. Box 840, Kennebunkport, ME. 04046 (207) 967-5595. ***Isle of Shoals Steamship Co.,** Box 311 (315 Market St), Portsmouth, NH. 03802 1-800-441-4620.

The following lighthouses are included in the Maine Lights Program:

Browns Head Light	Egg Rock Light	Little River Light	Ram Island Ledge Light
Burnt Island Light	Fort Point Light	Marshall Point Light	Rockland Breakwater Light
Cape Neddick Light	Goat Island Light	Matinicus Rock Light	Seguin Island Light
Curtis Island Light	Goose Rocks Light	Monhegan Island Light	Spring Point Ledge Light
Deer Is. Thorofare(Mark Is.) Light	Gt. Duck Is. Light	Moose Peak Light	Two Bush Island Light
Doubling Point Light	Halfway Rock Light	Mt. Desert Rock Light	West Quoddy Head Light
Kennebec River Range Lights	Isle au Haut Light	Nash Island Light	Whitehead Island Light
Eagle Island Light	Libby Island Light	Ram Island Light	Whitlocks Mill & Wood Is. Lights

Organizations/Museums:

**The U.S. Lighthouse Society offers a tour of Maine lighthouses each fall, which includes lights from Portland Head to Penobscot Bay: *244 Kearney St., 5th Floor, San Francisco, CA. 94108, (415) 362-7255.*

**American Lighthouse Foundation is a volunteer organization dedicated to the history, preservation and restoration of lighthouses *P.O. Box 889, Wells, ME. 04090.*

**The Friends of Seguin *P.O. Box 438, Georgetown, ME. 04548*-- or contact the *Maine Maritime Museum in Bath, ME.* for additional information.

**Friends of Acadia (preservation and restoration of Baker Island Lighthouse) *P.O. Box 725, Bar Harbor, ME. 04609*

**Friends of Nubble Light, *Box 9, c/o York Recreation and Parks Office, York, ME. 03909*

**Marshall Point Lighthouse Museum, *P.O. Box 247, Port Clyde, ME. 04855.* Located in the keeper's house and recently restored kitchen building at Marshall Point Light. Open daily June through September (1-5pm), weekends during May and October.

**The Fisherman's Museum (at Pemaquid Point Lighthouse); historical information and displays of the region's fishing and maritime industry. *Pemaquid Point Rd., New Harbor, ME. 04554.* Open Memorial Day through Columbus Day.

**Shore Village Museum: A comprehensive and impressive collection of lighthouse equipment, historical records and artifacts, including a variety of classical lenses, assembled by Ken Black. *104 Limerock St., Rockland, ME. 04841.* Open June to mid-October.

**Portland Harbor Museum, (at Southern Maine Technical College) *Fort Rd., So. Portland, ME   04106*

**Friends of Rockland Breakwater Light, *PO Box 741, Rockland, ME. 04841*

LIGHTHOUSE	COLOR	CHARACTERISTIC	DESCRIPTION
East Quoddy Head	Red	Fixed	
Whitlocks Mill	Green	Equal 6 second intervals, light & dark	Height above water: 32 ft Range: 5nm
Mulholland (inactive)	NA	NA	NA
West Quoddy Head	White	Group flashing white 15 seconds	Height above water: 83 ft Range: 18nm
Lubec Channel	White	Flashing 6 seconds	Height above water: 53 ft Range: 6nm
Little River (Inactive)	NA	NA	NA
Machias Seal Island	White	Flashing 3 seconds	Height above water: 82 ft Range: 17 nm
Libby Island	White	Group flashing 20 seconds	Height above water: 91 ft Range: 25 nm
Moose Peak	White	Flashing 30 seconds	Height above water: 72 ft Range: 26 nm
Nash Island (inactive)	NA	NA	NA
Narraguagus (Pond) Is. (inactive)	NA	NA	NA
Petit Manan Island	White	Flashing 10 seconds	Height above water: 123 ft Range: 26nm
Prospect Harbor	Red with 2	Flashing 6 seconds	Height above water: 42 ft Range: Red=7nm; White=9nm
Winter Harbor (Mark Is.) (inactive)	NA	NA	NA
Egg Rock	Red	Flashing 5 seconds	Height above water: 64 ft Range: 14nm
Bear Island- (private aid)	White	Flashing 5 seconds	Height above water: 100ft
Baker Island	White	Flashing 10 seconds	Height above water: 105 ft Range: 10nm
Mt. Desert Rock	White	Flashing 15 seconds	Height above water: 75 ft Range: 18nm
Great Duck Island	Red	Flashing 5 seconds	Height above water: 67 ft Range: 19nm
Bass Harbor Head	Red	Occulting 4 seconds	Height above water: 56 ft Range: 13nm
Burnt Coat Harbor (Hockamock Head)	White	Occulting 4 seconds	Height above water: 75 ft Range: 9 nm
Blue Hill Bay (inactive)	NA	NA	NA
Saddleback Ledge	White	Flashing 6 seconds	Height above water: 54ft Range: 11nm
Isle au Haut	Red with white sector	Flashing 4 seconds	Height above water: 48 ft Range: Red=6nm; white=8nm
Eagle Island	White	Flashing 4 seconds	Height above water: 106 ft Range: 9nm
Mark Island / Deer Isle Thorofare	White	Flashing 6 seconds	Height above water: 52 ft Range: 9nm
Pumpkin Island (inactive)	NA	NA	NA
Dyce Head (inactive)	NA	NA	NA
Fort Point (Stockton Springs)	White	Fixed	Height above water:88 ft Range: 15nm
Grindle Point	Green	Flashing 4 seconds	Height above water:39 ft Range: 6nm
Curtis Island	Green	Fixed	Height above water: 52 ft Range: 6nm
Indian Island (inactive)	NA	NA	NA
Goose Rocks	Red with white sector	Flashing red 6 seconds	Height above water: 51 ft Range: Red=11nm; White=12nm
Browns Head	White with 2 red sectors	Fixed	Height above water:39 ft Range: Red=11nm; White=14nm
Rockland Breakwater	White	Flashing 5 seconds	Height above water:39 ft Range: 17nm
Matinicus Rock	White	Flashing 10 seconds	Height above water: 90 ft Range: 20nm

LIGHTHOUSE	COLOR	CHARACTERISTIC	DESCRIPTION
Heron Neck	Red with white sector	Fixed	Height above water: 92 ft Range: Red=10nm;white=13nm
Two Bush Island	White with red sector	Flashing white 5 seconds	Height above water: 65 ft Range: Red=18nm;white=22nm
Owl's Head	White	Fixed	Height above water: 100 ft Range: 16 nm
Marshall Point	White	Fixed	Height above water: 30 ft Range: 13 nm
Whitehead Island	Green	Occulting 4 seconds	Height above water: 75 ft Range: 10 nm
Tenants Harbor (Inactive)	NA	NA	NA
Franklin Island	White	Flashing 6 seconds	Height above water: 57 ft Range: 8 nm
Pemaquid Point	White	Flashing 6 seconds	Height above water: 79 ft Range: 14 nm
Monhegan Island	White	Flashing 30 seconds	Height above water: 178 ft Range: 21nm
Ram Island	Red with 2 white sectors	Fixed	Height above water: 36ft Range: Red=9nm;white=11nm
Burnt Island	Red with 2 white sectors	Red flashing 6 seconds	Height above water: 61 ft Range:Red=12nm;white=15nm
Cuckholds	White	Group flashing twice every 6 seconds	Height above water: 59 ft Range: 12nm
Hendricks Head	White with red sector	Fixed	Height above water: 43 ft Range: Red=7nm;white=9nm
Seguin Island	White	Fixed	Height above water: 180 ft Range: 18nm
Pond Island	White	Equal 6 second intervals, light & dark	Height above water: 52 ft Range: 9nm
Perkins Island	Red with 2 white sectors	Flashing red 2.5 seconds	Height above water: 41ft Range: Red=5nm; white=6nm
Squirrel Point	Red with white sector	Equal interval red 6 seconds	Height above water: 25 ft Range: Red=7nm; white=9nm
Kennebec River Range Lights	Front=White Rear= White	Front=continuous quick flash Rear= Equal interval white 6 seconds	Height above water: Front=18 ft, Rear= 33 ft
Doubling Point	White	Flashing 4 seconds	Height above water: 23 ft Range: 9 nm
Halfway Rock	Red	Flashing 5 seconds	Height above water: 77 ft Range: 19 nm
Ram Island Ledge	White	Group flashing 6 seconds	Height above water: 77 ft Range: 12 nm
Portland Breakwater (Inactive)	NA	NA	NA
Spring Point Ledge	White with 3 red sectors	Flashing white 6 seconds	Height above water: 54 ft Range: Red=9nm;white=12nm
Portland Head	White	Flashing 4 seconds	Height above water: 101 ft Range: 24 nm
Cape Elizabeth (Two Lights)	White	Group flashing white	Height above water: 129 ft Range: 15 nm
Wood Island	White & green	Alternating 10 seconds	Height above water: 71 ft Range: White=16nm;green=14nm
Goat Island	White	Flashing 6 seconds	Height above water: 38 ft Range: 12 nm
Cape Neddick (Nubble)	Red	Equal interval 6 seconds	Height above water: 88 ft Range: 13nm
Boon Island	White	Flashing white 5 seconds	Height above water: 137 ft Range: 19 nm
Whaleback	White	Group flashing twice every 10 seconds	Height above water: 59 ft Range: 24 nm
Portsmouth Harbor	Green	Fixed	Height above water: 52 ft Range: 12 nm
White Island	White	Flashing 15 seconds	Height above water: 82 ft Range: :20nm

Index

Seguin Island Light

CatNap Publications
P.O. Box 848
Mt. Desert, ME.   04660